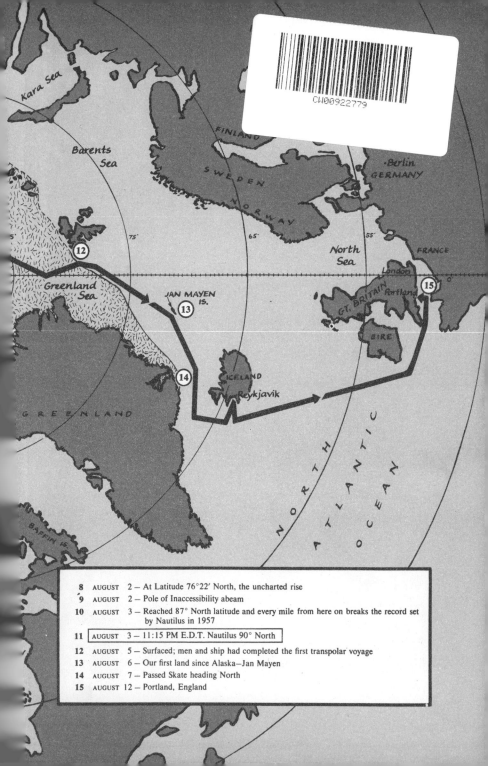

CW00922779

8 AUGUST 2 — At Latitude 76°22′ North, the uncharted rise
9 AUGUST 2 — Pole of Inaccessibility abeam
10 AUGUST 3 — Reached 87° North latitude and every mile from here on breaks the record set by Nautilus in 1957
11 AUGUST 3 — 11:15 PM E.D.T. Nautilus 90° North
12 AUGUST 5 — Surfaced; men and ship had completed the first transpolar voyage
13 AUGUST 6 — Our first land since Alaska—Jan Mayen
14 AUGUST 7 — Passed Skate heading North
15 AUGUST 12 — Portland, England

NAUTILUS 90 NORTH

NAVSHIPS 1111 (REV. 11-54)

SHIP'S POSITION

U. S. S. _NAUTILUS_

TO: COMMANDING OFFICER

AT (Time of day) 1915 U		DATE 3 August 1958	
LATITUDE 90° 00.0'N	LONGITUDE Indefinite	DETERMINED AT —	

BY (Indicate by check in box)
[X] N6A ~~CELESTIAL~~   [X] D. R.   [X] MK19 ~~LORAN~~   [ ] RADAR   [ ] VISUAL

SET —	DRIFT —	DISTANCE MADE GOOD SINCE (time) (miles) Honolulu 4844	
DISTANCE TO North Pole		MILES Zero	ETA —

TRUE HDG. 180°	ERROR MK19 GYRO 3°E MK23 GYRO 0°	VARIATION 170° E

MAGNETIC COMPASS HEADING (Check one)
[ ] STD   [ ] STEERING   [X] REMOTE IND   [ ] OTHER   M 244   G 359 °

DEVIATION 126E	1104 TABLE DEVIATION 3° W	DG: (Indicate by check in box) [ ] ON [X] OFF

REMARKS

NGA DR
$\sigma = 0$
$N = 0$

N6A
$n_x = 0$
$n_y = 0$
$n_z = 1$

RESPECTFULLY SUBMITTED (Navigator)
LT Shepherd M. Jenks, USN

CC:

A-32799

NAUTILUS
—90—
NORTH

by

COMMANDER WILLIAM R. ANDERSON,
U.S.N.

with Clay Blair, Jr.

London
HODDER AND STOUGHTON

Copyright © 1959 by William R. Anderson and Clay Blair, Jr.

MADE AND PRINTED IN GREAT BRITAIN FOR
HODDER AND STOUGHTON LIMITED, LONDON
BY C. TINLING AND CO. LIMITED, LIVERPOOL
LONDON AND PRESCOT

Foreword

By Rear-Admiral G. B. H. Fawkes, C.B., C.V.O., C.B.E.

Flag Officer Submarines and Commander Submarines Eastern Atlantic (NATO) 1954-55

There is a brotherhood between submariners of all nations, but none so firm as that between the American and British submariners.

During two commissions in the Far East before World War II, I had the good fortune to get to know many American submariners. My flotilla was based at Hong Kong, the Americans in Manila, but two or three times a year we would meet, visit each other's "boats," have the most tremendous parties and discuss our role in a future war. In the Far East in those days, the British submarines were the most modern ocean patrol submarines we had, the American submarines were old and small.

Who could have foreseen that in a few years' time, the British large ocean-going submarines, practically all of this type that we had, would be withdrawn from the Far East and sent mostly to the Mediterranean to meet the urgent needs for submarines in that theatre? Who could have foreseen that the Far East would become practically the exclusive submarine hunting-grounds of a vast number of the largest and most up-to-date American ocean patrol submarines?

Towards the end of World War II, we did indeed send British submarines out to the Far East but, by that time, our pre-war large submarines had mostly been lost in the Mediterranean and our war-time submarine construction was rightly concentrated on the smaller general purpose types, primarily designed to operate in the face of concentrated enemy anti-submarine measures in the relatively confined waters of the

North Sea and Mediterranean. They could and did operate in the Atlantic and Pacific, but they could only be effective for a much shorter period than their American larger brothers.

British submarines sank nearly two million tons of enemy shipping in World War II, mostly in the Mediterranean and North Sea, but at a loss of some seventy of their number. If we were the experts in the small submarine field, the Americans were even more so in the large long-distance submarine. They sank nearly four million tons of enemy shipping in the Pacific.

It is only fitting therefore that the truly remarkable exploit of Nautilus, so modestly yet so vividly described in this book, should have been carried out by an American submarine, and I am sure the British submariner is as proud of this feat as is his American brother.

It was my great honour as well as my most stimulating pleasure in my capacity as Commander Submarines Eastern Atlantic, to have a great insight into the post-war affairs of American submarines. We planned together, we operated together under the ægis of NATO and we had a mutual regard for each other's problems and aspirations.

One day in 1955 in Pearl Harbour, Honolulu, the main Pacific submarine base, I had the good fortune to discuss with Admiral Rickover, the father of the nuclear-powered submarine, some of his views on the future that lay ahead for these craft.

During one of my several visits to New London, the home of the American Atlantic submariner, I was able to see at close quarters both Nautilus and her younger sister Seawolf at their moorings and I so well remember Admiral Watkins' (Commanding American Atlantic submarines) genuine disappointment that his hoped-for special permission for me to visit them could not be granted. That permission has since been granted by Congress to my successors as well as to other British experts concerned in the construction of Dreadnought, our first nuclear-powered submarine to be.

The Nautilus' feat could only be achieved by a nuclear propelled submarine. No other submarine can achieve anything approaching such a sustained high speed. The conventional submarine must surface or stick its "snort" breathing tube above water to enable its diesel engines to recharge its electric batteries. This slows the submarine down very considerably and, where there is ice, is obviously impossible.

Given nuclear propulsion and the most modern methods of air conditioning and purification, the feat of the Nautilus was still far from easy and certainly not without hazard.

The earlier chapters of this book describe the preliminary probes that had to be made under the ice cap and the special equipment that was needed to make such an operation possible.

The most hazardous features of this great exploit were the attempts to penetrate the shallow Bering Strait, where the under-side of the ice pack almost touches the sea bed!

This remarkable feat may be considered by many to be "fan-damn-tastic" to use a Nautilus adjective, but in no sense can it be regarded as only a spectacular and otherwise worthless stunt.

Not only did this epic voyage open up the North-West passage, the shortest route from Europe to the Pacific, for submarine vessels of the future, but most important, to my mind, it presents us with an entirely new field for strategic operations in the northernmost part of the Atlantic with all its vast implications for the future.

Submarine liners and cargo ships of the future (and who can doubt but that they will be built?) may be able in a certain period of the year to make the North-West passage, though the hazards so vividly described may continue to rule this out except as an operation of war.

Most significant of all is the fact that Nautilus has proved that nuclear-powered submarines can operate in an area where no surface ships or aircraft can attack them.

Using the now accurate inertia system of navigation and selecting any one of the many ice-free stretches of water that surprisingly exist in the north polar cap, the nuclear-powered and ballistic-missile-armed submarine may well prove to be the most powerful weapon of the future. We should indeed be thankful that our American friends and Allies have pioneered this outstanding achievement.

Barney Fawkes

10th November, 1958

Contents

List of Illustrations

Except where otherwise acknowledged all the
illustrations in this book are from official U.S.
Navy photographs

NAUTILUS 90 NORTH

ONE

"Execute Operation *Sunshine*"

It was Sunday, June 8, 1958. Our ship, the nuclear-powered submarine Nautilus, lay quietly moored at Pier 91 in Seattle, Washington. The waters lapped gently against the sleek hull and against the sides of the many surface ships tied up near us. Large, billowy cumulus clouds banked overhead; sea-gulls swooped and cawed, seeking an afternoon repast. Our star-flecked Union Jack flapped lazily on its mast at the bow. All in all, I imagined, the small segment of the world which Nautilus dominated was a model of Sunday serenity.

Yet, for me, the moment was far from serene. It was a time of mental anguish such as I have rarely experienced. Sitting at my desk behind the locked door of my small stateroom, I restlessly downed one cup of black coffee after another. My eyes, strained from lack of sleep, kept wandering toward the bulkhead clock. It was 2:00 P.M. Seattle time. I had yet to receive a final Top Secret word from Washington which would tell us whether Nautilus would return to routine operations or embark upon one of the most dramatic, historic, and challenging sea voyages of all time.

Lying before me on my desk were two sets of operational orders. One bore the label "Confidential". It directed Nautilus to make a long, routine, submerged transit to Panama for the collection of data in support of Polaris submarine operations. The other set of orders, which until that moment I had kept in a triple-lock safe, was stamped "Top Secret—Eyes Only of the Commanding Officer". The Top Secret orders stated that, if directed by the Chief of Naval Operations, we should ignore previous instructions and proceed to Portland, England, not by the usual route, but beneath the vast Arctic ice pack which lies atop the globe.

Only a handful of people on Nautilus and in Washington knew of the existence of the Top Secret orders. They had received the personal attention and approval of the Commander in Chief, President Dwight D. Eisenhower. The responsibility for the decision to execute the Top Secret orders—to launch Operation SUNSHINE, as it was called—rested with the Chief of Naval Operations, Admiral Arleigh Burke. It was his word, or the word of his Deputy for Operations, Vice Admiral Thomas S. Combs, that I awaited.

The crew of Nautilus knew nothing of the momentous— indeed dazzling—implications of the Top Secret orders. At that moment they were busily making last-minute preparations to get under way for a southern voyage. I had filed a routine movement report giving a routing to, and a destination of, Panama. My Executive Officer, Lieutenant Commander Frank Adams, a lanky, soft-spoken Mississippian, and I had accepted a dinner engagement in Panama for the evening of July 3. Nautilus crewmen were looking forward to picking up gifts in Panamanian shops on which they had left deposits when we passed through the Canal two months earlier.

Our nuclear engine, which requires no air and thus would make a long trip beneath the ice pack theoretically feasible, was in tip-top condition. At that point, it had driven Nautilus faultlessly over 115,000 miles, most of it beneath the sea, and with only one refuelling. Many thousands of miles of steaming were available to us before the next refuelling. Nautilus was, without reservation, a proven application of nuclear power.

Even so, the man who designed and built the power plant, Rear Admiral H. G. Rickover,* continued to maintain an overriding interest in the ship. As one of the few who knew of the possibility of Operation SUNSHINE, he was particularly

---

*In October, 1958, "the father of the atomic submarine" was promoted to the rank of Vice Admiral.

Daily Mail

Commander William R. Anderson, captain of Nautilus.

The triumphal return to New London, Connecticut, after the trans-polar voyage. "Panopos," derived from "the Pacific to the Atlantic via the North Pole," was the nickname given to the crew.

Mrs. Dwight D. Eisenhower christens Nautilus in January 1954.

WELCOME HOME PANOPOS

concerned that the power plant be in peak condition. During
our time in Seattle, we had been in almost daily contact with
the Admiral by telephone, keeping him posted on every facet of
the plant. No detail escaped his probing, long-distance inspection.

That day, as I awaited final word, Admiral Rickover flew in
from Washington for a personal inspection. In his usual dyn-
amic, inquisitive manner, he toured the plant, shot-gunning
questions to the engineers. He stood by while the Engineering
Officer, Lieutenant Commander Paul Early, one of the best
nuclear engineers in the business, conducted the multitudinous
checks that determine the readiness of the reactor to be placed
in operation, or, as we put it, "to go critical". When he was
certain that everything was in order—the plant was performing
as well as, or better than, it ever had—Admiral Rickover and I
returned to my stateroom. As he sat down on the edge of my
bunk, I locked the door and withdrew a polar chart from my
safe. I briefly traced the route that I intended to follow, should
SUNSHINE become a reality. I scribbled a rough schedule on the
chart—showing arrival times at the edge of the ice pack, at the
North Pole, and at the expected termination of our under-ice
travels in the Greenland Sea. Long before, I had committed
two sets of figures to memory—one, the optimistic schedule I
hoped to make good; the other, the schedule I would show to
the few entitled to know, a conservative schedule which would
guarantee that even appreciable delays would not cause worry.
The latter were the figures I used on Admiral Rickover's chart,
which I folded and shoved into an envelope already marked
"Top Secret". As he wedged the envelope into his bulging
brief-case, the Admiral told me of extreme methods I could
use to operate the reactor, should we have difficulties under
ice. I knew he was telling me, in effect, to accept serious
damage to the propulsion plant rather than risk the ship and
the crew.

Then as he rose to go, he asked, as is always his custom, if
there was anything he could do for me. I thought of but one
thing. I had recently been presented with a handsome gold

B

wrist watch by the Navy League of the United States. I asked if he would, on his return to Washington, send it to my wife.

Just an hour after Admiral Rickover's departure, I went in to Nautilus' commodious Wardroom and spoke quietly into the ear of Captain J. C. Dempsey, Commander Submarine Flotilla One, and our West Coast operational boss.

"Well, sir," I said, "I guess the time has come."

Together we put in a telephone call to Rear Admiral L. R. Daspit, the Navy Department's Director of Undersea Warfare, top submarine boss in the Pentagon. We reached the Admiral at his home in Washington. Our message was brief: "Nautilus is ready to go." There was a momentary silence. I waited in agony, thinking, *No ship has ever been so ready to accomplish a mission. Surely there can be no word but to proceed northward.*

After what seemed like an eternity—and here that shopworn phrase can be used with full sincerity and accuracy—Admiral Daspit replied, "Execute Operation Sunshine." It was England! Via the polar pack and the North Pole!

Despite having been preoccupied with Operation Sunshine for months on end, I had replaced the phone in its cradle before the full impact of Admiral Daspit's words struck me. My reaction was not one of surprise. In its long history, the Navy has seldom hesitated to launch bold and daring operations, either in war or peace. Frankly, I was engulfed by a feeling of relief. The gnawing anxiety which had plagued me, that for one reason or another the trip might be cancelled, was gone. Had I the ability to see what lay ahead, that Nautilus would soon experience the narrowest escape in her history, that the lives of all men on board would be in dire peril, I might have been less enthusiastic. But at that moment I was jubilant.

As I said goodbye to Captain Dempsey, I reflected on the chain of events that had brought Nautilus and me to the threshold of our great adventure. Many things rushed to mind. My first interview with Admiral Rickover. The great luck of being assigned command of the Nautilus. Our first, hair-raising probe of the Arctic ice pack the year before. The fantastic cloak-and-dagger prelude to Operation SUNSHINE itself. The dramatic and vexing events on board Nautilus during the previous two months, which, it seemed to me, were clear signals from a higher Person, that we should stop tempting fate —give up plans for Operation SUNSHINE.

I had a feeling that it could not possibly be true. Yet it was.

TWO

A Difficult Interview

My role in the momentous transpolar voyage of the Nautilus began on a chilly, overcast January day in 1956. At that time I was in charge of instruction in submarine combat tactics at the United States Submarine School in New London, Connecticut.

New London is a kind of second home and common meeting ground for submariners. Most submariners—enlisted men and officers alike—receive their first training there. Sooner or later most submariners wind up in New London on a tour of duty, either at the school, or on the staff of the Commander, Submarines, Atlantic Fleet, who maintains his headquarters on the base. The Electric Boat Division of General Dynamics, which has built more submarines for the Navy than any other concern, is located only a few miles down-river from the base. Many submarines put into New London or Electric Boat for overhaul, repairs, and modification.

What for me began as a routine day in a strictly routine job was soon upset by a telephone call from Rear Admiral Frank Watkins, Commander, Submarines, Atlantic, asking that I come immediately to his office.

When I reported in, the Admiral invited me to sit down for a cup of coffee. Then, in a very informal manner and without revealing his purpose, he began asking about my past duty in submarines. I gave him a thumbnail sketch: eleven war patrols in World War II on the Tarpon, Narwhal, and Trutta, post-war duty on Sarda, Trutta, Tang, and finally, in 1953, my own command, the new fast attack submarine, Wahoo. I served aboard Wahoo for two years, operating from Hawaii and

Japan, before reporting in for duty at the Submarine School.

When I had completed my summary, the Admiral, in a tone that clearly indicated the mysterious interview was finished, said, "Very well. There is someone coming into town that I may want you to meet and talk with. Where can you be reached by telephone tonight?"

"I will be at home," I said. I left the Admiral's office completely baffled.

I lived with my wife, Bonny, and our two sons, Michael, eleven, and Bill, six months, in the nearby seaport village of Mystic, Connecticut. Our house was a rambling antique of colonial days, comfortable but not pretentious. I went home late that day, all the while trying to figure who it might be the Admiral wanted me to see. After dinner that evening, the Admiral called.

"I'm sorry to say that the man's schedule was overcrowded," Admiral Watkins said. "He won't be able to see you this trip."

"Aye, aye, sir," I said.

The Admiral must have guessed that I was bursting with curiosity, because he added in a low, confidential tone:

"Don't say anything about this. The man I'm talking about is Admiral Rickover. There is an important job coming up and you are being considered as a possibility, along with some other people."

"Yes, sir, Admiral. I understand."

Then, after instructing me to make plans to go to Washington for an interview with Admiral Rickover, Admiral Watkins rang off.

I collapsed in a chair, literally stunned.

By then, of course, everyone in the submarine force knew either directly or indirectly of Rear Admiral H. G. Rickover, the "father of the atomic submarine". The Nautilus, launched in January 1954, had been operating almost a full year. Her performance and reliability had electrified submariners the world over, and especially all of us at New London. We were already aware that the ship was revolutionizing naval warfare. To us she was truly sensational.

But, I thought, what kind of job could I do for Admiral Rickover? I knew that his unique development organization in Washington was composed of specialists in physics, engineering, mathematics, shipbuilding, and reactor design. I had no special qualifications in any of those fields. In what way could I possibly contribute? I didn't know, but I could think of no place on earth where I would rather work. Against what I felt to be a remote possibility that he might actually offer me a job, I began making preparations and, incidentally, taking some precautions.

A few weeks later orders arrived, requesting that I report to Admiral Rickover's office at 0800 on a Saturday morning. I arrived in Washington on Friday evening and spent the night as the guest of a former skipper, Commander Enders P. Huey. I had just unpacked my travelling bag when the telephone jangled. The caller identified himself as a naval officer who worked for Admiral Rickover. He said he was sorry to report that the Admiral would be busy most of the day and there was no need for me to come over before late afternoon. I said, "Fine. Fine. Thank you," and hung up.

Within the Navy, "interviews" with Admiral Rickover are rather famous or, perhaps, infamous. Almost anything can happen. At one time, for example, the Admiral kept a special chair for interviewees, the front legs of which were shorter than its rear legs. It was always placed in such a position that, with an easy flick of the Venetian blinds, the Admiral could focus the bright rays of the sun in the interviewee's eyes. Many young naval officers sat in the chair blinded by the sun, sliding forward, all the while being pummelled by questions that had no easy answer or perhaps no answer at all.

The questions might assume any form. I had heard, for example, of the Admiral's interview with a young engineer. It was quite a well-known story in submarine circles.

"Are you resourceful?" the Admiral asked.

"Um—well, yes, sir," the engineer replied.

"Suppose you're on a sinking ship with five other men. The conditions are that one, and only one of you, can be saved. Are you resourceful enough to talk the other five into letting you be the one?"

The engineer, hardly aware that he might have to explain further, replied again. "Um—yes, sir."

The Admiral gave an almost imperceptible signal. Where-upon five men came into the room and arranged themselves around the engineer. "All right, son," said Rickover. "Start talking."

Once, I had heard, a young naval officer undergoing an interview was asked this question: "You are a naval officer. A situation has arisen where the citizens of Washington must decide to liquidate either you or the man who keeps the city's streets clean. If you lived in Washington, which one would you rather have eliminated?"

The young lad, suspecting that Rickover was probing for a show of modesty, answered promptly, "Myself, of course, sir."

"If so," the Admiral said, crashing his fist on the top of his desk, "that's the wrong answer."

Then he explained: "Don't you see that the proper man to eliminate is the street cleaner? The reason for this is that you— the naval officer—can be a street cleaner, too, but the street cleaner cannot be a naval officer unless he's trained."

Rickover's tricky questions, I knew, were not designed to embarrass or belittle the prospective candidate, but rather to separate quickly the dull, orthodox thinkers from the quick-witted, resourceful men whom the Admiral gathers close around him, and above all, to weed out those showing even a slight tendency toward dishonesty.

I was dead certain I could never outfox the Admiral, nor was I inclined to try, but I was determined to do everything in my power to make a good impression. Thus it was that after I had received that phone call delaying my appointment, I began to worry. Had the call been a Rickover ruse? My orders read that I should report at 0800. Perhaps, I thought, he was testing me to see if I could be persuaded to fail to follow orders by a phone call from someone I did not know. I then made up my mind that, call or no call, I would report as ordered at 0800. And I did.

As it turned out, the Admiral *was* busy all morning and early afternoon. I sat in an office down the hall from the Admiral's, waiting and watching with fascination the ant like activity going on around me. It appeared to me that no-one in the entire wing of the building ever walked. Everybody ran.

Finally my time came. The Admiral was ready. Hat in hand I entered his office. The Admiral, white-haired and wiry, dressed in civilian clothes, was alternately sitting and pacing behind his desk, telephone in hand, barking orders to some hapless engineer, all the while making notes on scratch pads. My eyes wandered around the office. It was like no Admiral's office I had ever seen. The floors were bare of rugs. The room was jammed with bookcases crammed with every book imaginable. The Admiral's desk, the conference desk, and the side tables were stacked high with papers, reports, models, unhung pictures, and other miscellaneous items. In truth, the place reminded me of a library room just vacated by a dozen students working on their theses.

On invitation I sat down, relieved to find that I had survived the first thirty seconds. I was prepared to eliminate the street cleaner, and had a way devised to talk the five men on the sinking ship to let me go first. The special chair was not then a part of the interview. However, I don't think it would have affected me. At that moment my chair, for all I knew, could have had no legs at all.

The Admiral fixed his piercing eyes on me. Without fanfare or other preliminaries, he snapped: "Where did you go to school?"

This, for me, is a rather complicated question. My father, David H. Anderson, whose ancestors had long tilled the soil of Tennessee, was likewise a farmer. During the Depression we moved about often, while he recouped from the 1929 crash and started his own lumber business. Therefore in my younger years I attended many different schools. My last two years of high school were spent at Columbia Military Academy in Columbia, Tennessee.

Rather deliberately, I began an explanation of these facts. The Admiral cut in:

"Anderson. I didn't ask you for your life history. I just want to know where you graduated from high school."

"Columbia Military Academy," I replied with a sinking feeling. Despite my determination to prevent it, the interview was clearly off to a bad start.

Although the Admiral had said he did not want my life history, in short order he had obtained most of it.

I was born on the farm at Bakerville, Tennessee, June 17, 1921, the youngest of three children. By the time I was six or seven, I had learned my chores, and how to find my way around my father's lumber mill. My childhood hobby, not unnaturally, was woodwork. When I was about ten, my father set up a shop for me, and soon I began to turn out such items as lawn chairs and tables, which I sold. Sometimes I worked on other projects. I built a couple of rowboats, which were launched in the small river that ran close to home. James Beckham, a boyhood friend, and I converted one of the rowboats into a crude submarine. We found that by covering over most of the deck we could turn the boat upside down and submerge it with air pockets inside that permitted us to breathe. Thus we played at being U-boat captains.

Perhaps the greatest construction achievement of all was a miniature Ferris wheel. The Ferris wheel was the pride of the neighbourhood until one design weakness became apparent. At the top of the turn, we discovered, the seats failed to adjust regularly. Quite frequently, in fact, the kids slid out, hanging for dear life to a crossbar as they careered through the arc to the ground. Under stern orders from all parents concerned, the Ferris wheel was dismantled.

There was no special military tradition in our family. At about the time I was eleven or twelve, my father suggested that I should consider going to West Point or Annapolis as a means of obtaining a fine education that he might not otherwise be able to afford. It was with this objective in mind that I spent my last two years of high school in a military academy. Having skipped an earlier grade, I remained at Columbia an extra year after graduating, to prepare for the stiff Academy examinations. I passed and entered the Naval Academy in 1939.

My performance at the Academy was about average. I was neither an athlete nor a brain. World War II broke out soon after we entered, and the class was accelerated. When I graduated in 1942, standing in about the middle of our class of six hundred men, I found that certain restrictions had been relaxed, and that Annapolis graduates were allowed to apply straight for submarine school. Our class had made one summer cruise—in 1940—on the battleships Texas, New York, and Arkansas, and I had come away with the impression that I would not like the spit and polish of a large ship. Because they were small and informal, and because responsibility would come sooner, submarines appealed to me. I put in an application and was lucky enough to be among the first forty Annapolis men selected directly for submarines.

At sea there is little in the life of a submariner that is, relatively speaking, routine. In wartime, as I soon found out, submarines, usually operating alone, spent many long weeks out of port, fearlessly stalking through enemy harbours and sea lanes, sinking ships, or evading tenacious enemy anti-submarine vessels. The mortality rate on submarines is high—higher than in any other branch of the service—and the restricted quarters can become uncomfortable. In peacetime, submarines rarely have a chance to rest. Usually there are not enough boats to go around, and those in commission maintain a busy schedule, operating in training exercises and teaching our own anti-submarine forces how to make a kill.

While seldom routine, the life of a submariner provides some intangible rewards. The most important of these is the privilege of associating with a group of men who, from the standpoint of courage, character, and boldness, have few equals. Many of these men, my friends and classmates, died on submarines in World War II. I was lucky. I survived. I was proud that I had played a small role in sending many Japanese vessels, including one of her largest troopships, to the bottom; prouder still to be a member in good standing of this splendid corps.

Between war patrols in World War II, on a ten-day leave back in the States in June 1943, I married Bonny, or Yvonne, Etzel, the daughter of a research chemist, Dr. Gastao Etzel. I was introduced to her by my room-mate at the Naval Academy, who was from Delaware. After graduating from the University of Delaware in Newark, she was, for a brief period, an airline stewardess. In March 1945, while I was at sea on war patrol on a new submarine I had helped to commission, I received word that our first son, Michael, had been born.

All of this, as I said, Admiral Rickover managed to extract from me. But the longer I talked, the more inadequate I felt, and the more my life seemed, in retrospect, about as unspectacular and humdrum as one could expect in the submarine service. Perhaps, I thought, that was why the Admiral had not bothered to ask me the tricky questions. Finally, he put this question to me:

"Anderson. Name the books and their authors that you have read in the last two years. Don't mention anything you have read within the past month. That doesn't count, because you had word you were coming down here."

During my tours at sea, it was my custom to take along a quantity of books of all kinds—novels, history, technical works, or whatever struck my fancy. I am not a prodigious reader but, I believe, I read far more than the average person. During sea operations on Wahoo, about the time of the Korean War wind-up, I had read, perhaps, two dozen books. But now I was struck completely dumb. For the life of me I couldn't remember a single title or author.

A scene flooded into my mind. It was in 1934. I was thirteen years old, graduating from grammar school in Waynesboro. I had been selected to be class valedictorian or salutatorian—I don't recall which. A friend of the family, something of a poet and philosopher, had written a short speech for me, which was full of big words and phrases. I spent three days memorizing that speech. Then came the big day. I walked out on the stage to the lectern, facing the crowd of proud mothers and fathers, including my own. Then I froze. My mind went blank. I was unable to remember a word of the speech. "Thank you," I said, and sat down.

Now, before Rickover, I had almost exactly the same feeling. I fumbled, recalling one book, the name of which I have now forgotten, but I could not remember the author's name. Rickover frowned. Then he said with finality:

"Goodbye."

I returned to my home in Mystic. Bonny could sense that all had not gone well. I confirmed her intuition: "What a situation! He asked the titles and authors of the books I had read in the last two years. I couldn't remember a single one. I don't know what job he had in mind, but I do know that I will never get it."

Later, perhaps instinctively, I wandered into our library. As I studied the rows of titles, I began to remember: "Here's one I read on Wahoo." With the help of my wife, I soon compiled a list of about twenty-four books that I had read, a list that represented about 90 per cent of my reading for the previous two years.

"Well," I said to Bonny, "this is probably useless and presumptuous, but just so he doesn't think every submarine officer is a total stupe, I am going to write and send him these titles." I sat down that very day and pecked the letter out on the typewriter. The next day, with some apprehension, I put it in the mail.

Although the Admiral has never told me directly, he has intimated that that letter was, as far as the interview was concerned, a turning point. Before he received it, Rickover had all but rejected me. He has said that at that time I appeared too calm and easy-going. After the letter arrived, he changed his mind. And shortly thereafter, to my astonishment, I received word that I should report to Admiral Rickover's office for duty. Just exactly what my "job" would be was not made clear, nor would it be for many months.

THREE

A "Hero" in NRB

My transfer from the Submarine Base at New London to Admiral Rickover's Naval Reactors Branch (NRB) in Washington became effective in July 1956. Soon after I arrived, I realized that, along with Commander Jim Calvert, I had been selected as a prospective commanding officer of a nuclear-powered submarine. No one ever said positively that I would receive such a command, but at least I was there as a "prospective candidate".

But which nuclear-powered submarine? Would it be one of the new boats—Skate, Swordfish, Skipjack? Or would it be the Nautilus? Captain Eugene P. Wilkinson had been skipper of the Nautilus for nearly two years. It seemed more likely to me that Nautilus would be the first billet open, yet I could not envision myself as skipper of this fabulous ship. It seemed like a fairy-tale. One day I put it to Admiral Rickover. He refused to comment directly.

"For purposes of training," he said, "let's assume it might be Nautilus."

I was assigned a small office in the battered temporary building which serves as the home of NRB. I studied and waited. And waited. All around me, engineers and scientists charged along at breakneck pace, wrestling with the baffling problems of reactor physics and steam-turbine systems. But no duties were assigned me. I was left sitting alone and unmolested at my bare desk. After a couple of days of this, I wandered into the maelstrom of the Admiral's office to remind him that I was aboard and to find out what I should do.

"Well, Anderson, suppose the first thing you do is sit down and write a memorandum to me proposing just what you ought to do."

"Aye, aye, sir," I said. I left his office in a hurry.

It was an interesting assignment. Just what should the prospective commanding officer of a nuclear-powered submarine study? Mathematics? Reactor physics? Chemistry? I had a few ideas, but I spent about a week talking with Rickover's top people, Harry Mandil, Ted Rockwell, Bob Panoff, and Captain James Dunford. Then I wrote a memorandum, based largely on their ideas, which included suggestions for several weeks at Arco, Idaho, to study the land-based prototype of the Nautilus plant, to Westinghouse, where the engines were built, to Electric Boat Company, where the submarines were under construction, along with a detailed study programme of the history of the project and of Nautilus operations to date. And finally, a detailed curriculum of self-study of the multitude of subjects embracing nuclear propulsion. The Admiral raised no objections to my plan. In fact, it became, for a time, a kind of standard programme for prospective commanding officers who came later.

The history of the project, I found, was stormy but fascinating. In 1946 Rickover, then a Captain, who had worked throughout World War II in the Bureau of Ships improving the electrical equipment on naval vessels, sought a post at the Atomic Energy Commission's Oak Ridge plant to study reactor physics. Three other naval officers. Lou Roddis, Jim Dunford, and Ray Dick, went along. In very short order, all four of these men had become fired with the idea of squeezing down the reactor, which was used to make plutonium, to a size small enough to fit into a submarine.

In principle, the concept was simple. The reactors at Oak Ridge were composed of uranium fuel rods, carefully spaced apart. When they were brought into proximity, a controlled reaction took place, as opposed to the uncontrolled reaction of the atomic bomb. Inside the reactor, the reaction generated enormous heat. To keep the heat within controllable bounds, engineers at Oak Ridge pumped water through the reactor. The water, in effect, entered one side of the reactor cold and exited through the other side boiling hot and, incidentally, radioactive. Rickover argued that if a means could be found to transfer the heat exiting from the reactor to another system, which itself would not become radioactive, then this heat, or energy, could be used to drive a steam-propulsion system.

Such a system in theory would be an ideal propulsion unit for a submarine, Rickover reasoned. It would burn only a minute quantity of fuel—a pound of uranium is equal to tens of thousands of gallons of conventional submarine Diesel oil. Equally important was the fact that since the "fire" in the reactor was not a chemical fire but rather a fission process, no outside air or oxygen would be required to sustain it. Submarines could do away with storage batteries—vastly increasing the space inside—and, in theory, remain submerged indefinitely. Jules Verne's dreams could come true!

From a practical, or engineering, standpoint, Rickover's concept threw many people into uncontrollable spasms of laughter. First, there was the stupendous problem of reducing the size of the reactor—the ones at Oak Ridge cover a couple of city blocks—to fit inside a submarine. Next, a system of transferring the heat from the radioactive, closed-water circuit revolving through the reactor to the normal steam-turbine system would have to be devised. Inside the radioactive portion of the water system, pumps would be required which could operate indefinitely without corroding or breaking down, because there would be no means of repairing them. Immensely heavy shielding would have to be provided for the reactor itself.

For three years Rickover, spurned and relegated to office space converted from a ladies' powder room, relentlessly pounded on desks, wrote letters, manoeuvred, sweated, and cursed, seeking a sympathetic ear. The Admiral has said:

"A military organization is set up to do routine, not imaginative work. If anyone comes along with a new idea, the people

Nautilus under way on the surface.

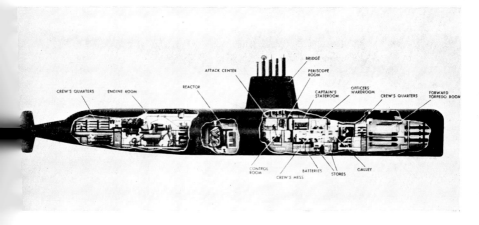

Cutaway view of Nautilus.

Aerial view of the Arctic ice pack.

At the edge of the ice pack on the 1957 cruise.

in the organization naturally tend to make him conform. The first thing a man has to do is make up his mind that he is going to get his head chopped off ultimately. If he has that feeling, perhaps he can accomplish something."

Rickover laid his head on the block. He wrote a letter direct to the Chief of Naval Operations, who was at that time Admiral Chester Nimitz, proposing the nuclear-powered submarine. Very shortly, and probably to his great surprise, he was appointed to head a new section in the Bureau of Ships called the Nuclear Power Division.

From long years of experience with Washington bureaucracy, Rickover knew this was not enough. The Atomic Energy Commission, which kept a tight watch on the United States uranium supply, was moving slowly in the development of practical nuclear power. At first, Rickover tried a frontal assault, blasting the agency through the lips of a co-operative admiral. Then his foxy mind conceived what has been described by one writer as a "classic manoeuvre in anti-bureaucracy". He persuaded the Atomic Energy Commission to form a Naval Reactors Branch and to name himself as its chief.

"Super-efficient 'administrators,'" Rickover says, "are the curse of the country. Their main function seems to be to harass brainworkers with trivia and to waste as much time as possible." In one ingenious stroke, Rickover had by-passed all administrators. As head of both the Navy and AEC divisions of the same project, he could, in effect, write himself letters, obtaining instant concurrence between both agencies on a contemplated programme. No longer would it be necessary for him to route letters up through the labyrinthine Navy chain of command and then back down the labyrinthine AEC chain to the proper individual, and wait several weeks for a reply to make its way through the same tortuous route. It could be done in a matter of seconds, and whatever Rickover wanted, Rickover got.

Meanwhile, to form the kind of resourceful team needed to push through such a revolutionary project, Rickover inter-

c

viewed more than a thousand engineers. Dissatisfied with
the general quality he encountered, he established a formal
nuclear engineering school, and began a crusade for better
education for gifted children, a crusade which continues to
this day.

With money and manpower at hand, the first designs of the
nuclear engine began to take shape on the drawing boards in
NRB. In an incredibly short time a full-size, land-based prototype of the submarine nuclear power plant was in operation,
inside an authentic submarine hull, at the AEC's desert test
centre in Arco, Idaho. Shortly thereafter, the Nautilus was
launched and put to sea; then came the Seawolf, with a different
engine design.

By the time I came on the scene in 1956, NRB had been in
formal operation for seven years; Rickover had been pushing
the nuclear-powered submarine concept for ten years. The
Admiral's top engineering team—Rockwell, Mandil, Panoff,
and others—were busy planning cheaper, more advanced
submarine reactors, and had begun work on nuclear engines
for an aircraft carrier, a cruiser, and a destroyer. The concept
of a missile-firing, nuclear-powered submarine, perhaps the
deadliest deterrent of the decade, was well along. As a side
project, Rickover and his team were building the United
States' first full-scale, nuclear-powered generating plant for
commercial power.

One's first glimpse into the inner workings and achievements
of this amazing group is awesome. There is no other way to
put it.

Quite naturally, however, it was Nautilus that interested
me most. I read through Captain Wilkinson's reports, and I
studied what the Navy's operational experts had to say.

Nautilus had got under way for the first time on January 17,
1955, at the Electric Boat Company in Groton, Connecticut.
From the bridge she signalled this momentous message:
"Under way on nuclear power." The ship crept slowly from the
dock, but after she was in the clear there was nothing slow
about Nautilus. At sea on trial runs, her performance astonished

even the men who had designed and built her. She could travel at a sustained underwater speed above twenty knots indefinitely. On her shakedown cruise she had travelled 1,381 miles entirely submerged in 89.9 hours, establishing what was then a remarkable submarine record. She was highly manoeuvrable underwater, could submerge to a very great depth, and in exercises with anti-submarine forces she proved herself fifty times as effective as a conventional submarine. Her power plant generated over twice as much mileage per unit of uranium as even the most optimistic forecasts.

I was soon swept up in the programme of learning in detail how Nautilus' reactor worked, travelling to Arco, and the Electric Boat and Westinghouse plants. I found my pace increasing, until soon I was following NRB's routine 8:00 to 5:30, six-day week, with many hours of additional homework at night. No one in NRB is required to move at this pace. Everyone just naturally falls in behind Rickover and tries to keep up. The Admiral is instinctively one of the greatest leaders I have ever known. No one in NRB is ever ordered to do anything. All major decisions are made by a panel of Rickover's top experts. He inspires intense loyalty in the men and women around him.

Admiral Rickover is frequently pictured as an impatient, ruthless, tough-minded intellectual, who believes that the shortest distance between two points is a line that bisects six admirals. I have seen him like that. He is that way when some "super-efficient administrator" raises some nit-picking point that might delay one of his projects, or when, as frequently happens, someone in one of the bureaux jumps on one of his men. In private, I found Rickover, after I came to know him, one of the most gentle, warm-hearted, and unselfish men I have ever met. And one with a keen sense of humour, too.

After I had been on board for several weeks, Rickover began calling all the prospective commanding officers "heroes," possibly to temper our cockiness, or at least to keep our heads from swelling when we contemplated the important assignments which lay ahead. Memorandums were actually routed to us labelled "Heroes".

One day a Wave lieutenant named Sally Higgins, a very talented singer, stopped by the Admiral's office on some errand. Since the resourceful Rickover is quick to learn any visitor's weak and strong points, he discovered in a short time that the Wave had a fine, even professional, voice. On the spot the Admiral asked her to sing for him. She did—the name of the song I have forgotten.

Then Admiral Rickover said, "Well, you've done enough for me. But I've got some heroes down the hall. I would like it very much if you would go down there and sing to them 'My Hero'. And by the way, since they are heroes, you had better take off your shoes before you go into their offices." Sally Higgins followed her instructions, and her monthly singing—in her stocking feet—of "My Hero" became an NRB ritual.

One of my fondest memories of NRB was the day Rickover was requested by the Chief of Naval Operations to wear a uniform at a certain luncheon they were both scheduled to attend. I've seen ships go through some emergencies, but I've never seen anything like the emergency that took place in Rickover's office when his girls tried to get together a proper uniform. By the time I arrived on the scene—I just happened by—everything was wrong. The ribbons were on the wrong side of the uniform, the cap cover did not match. The Admiral, who habitually wears civilian clothes, refused to have anything whatsoever to do with the preparations.

I jumped in and rearranged the ribbons, and changed the cap cover to match the uniform, for which, I am sure, the girls were very grateful. Later at lunch I was laughing with Captain Jim Dunford about the scene, and I commented, "You know, Jim, it's the first time I ever changed a cap cover for an admiral."

Jim's flashing eyes smiled over his cup of coffee. "Well, Andy, that's probably a good job for a commander!"

But by that time I knew positively that my job would be

command of Nautilus. Little did I dream then, however, that almost my entire period of command would be consumed with planning for, or actually probing beneath, the Arctic ice pack.

FOUR

An Unknown Quantity

The Arctic Ocean is an ice-covered body of water, five times the size of the Mediterranean Sea, lying atop our planet. Unlike the Antarctic area, which is mostly solid earth covered by ice and snow, the Arctic is completely fluid. The Arctic ice pack covering the ocean is not a totally solid layer of ice, as generally pictured, but rather it is composed of huge chunks and floes, varying greatly in size and thickness, grinding one upon the other, creating the effect of a solid mass. Here and there are leads, or cracks in the ice, and polynias, or fairly large open stretches, sometimes referred to as Arctic lagoons. The ice pack is in almost constant motion and in winter-time, in sub-zero weather, it reaches far down the coast of Greenland on the eastern side, and the Bering Strait on the western side.

It is a desolate, cold, barren, inhospitable place, which for decades has fascinated explorers, adventurers, and, more recently, defence experts, who visualize the Arctic as a possible battleground of the future.

In the fall of 1956 I knew no more than the average layman about the Arctic. If anyone had asked me point-blank, I could not have said whether the ice at the North Pole was four or four thousand feet thick. All that changed rather hurriedly one day, when I learned of a project being sponsored by a few officers in the Pentagon to send Nautilus to the Arctic the following summer.

I made a bee-line for the nearby Navy Department library. For me the research was far more than academic. Should such an expedition prove feasible, I would be commanding Nautilus, if all went well. Should it be a useless or foolhardy undertaking, I wanted to do everything in my power to stop it.

Day in and day out for the next several weeks, I read with complete fascination the accounts of men who had braved hardships to explore the Arctic. Many of these stories, such as Peary's trip across the ice to the Pole by sledge and Byrd's flight by airplane, are too well known to dwell upon here. What naturally interested me most were ship operations in the Arctic.

They were limited, I discovered, and most of them had ended in disaster. Some icebreakers had successfully bulldozed their way into the outer edge of the pack. Many others had failed. Two ships, the Norwegian Fram and the Russian Sedov, became locked in the ice and drifted helplessly, out of control, across the top of the world. Fram was stuck for thirty-five months and reached 85 degrees 57 minutes north latitude. (The North Pole is 90 degrees north.) The Sedov's trip was shorter, twenty-seven months, and it reached 86 degrees 39 minutes north latitude. In 1937 a handful of Russians landed a plane on an ice floe at the North Pole and drifted through the pack for nine months, until they reached open water near Greenland.

There had been few submarine operations in the Arctic area. The first and perhaps the most famous—but unsuccessful—was launched by Sir Hubert Wilkins in a ship also named Nautilus. Wilkins believed, on the basis of first-hand exploratory experience in the Arctic, that there were enough leads and polynias to enable a short-legged, battery-driven submarine to cross the ocean, by puddle-jumping beneath the ice and recharging batteries on the surface in open water. Believing the underside of the ice to be fairly smooth, he proposed to keep the submarine in a state of positive buoyancy—actually pushing up against the ice. Runners mounted topside like inverted skis would prevent damage to the ship itself. The propellers, of course, would provide the necessary propulsion.

The United States furnished Wilkins with a submarine that was scheduled for scrapping. The explorer fitted the ship out for under-ice operations, including devices with which he could drill through the ice in case the ship was trapped beneath it. The expedition set off amid a blizzard of publicity.

In August 1931, Wilkins' Nautilus reached the edge of the ice pack in the area between Spitsbergen and Greenland. Material failure, however, plagued the voyagers. It was soon discovered that the stern planes had been lost, making it difficult to submerge and control the ship. In spite of all this, several attempts were made to skid the submarine under the edge of the ice. Frost formed on the inside hull of the submarine and the crew became less than enthusiastic about the polar attempt. Finally, after some scientific data had been gathered on the edge of the pack, the expedition conceded defeat and headed south.

No submarine, to my knowledge, again came near the pack until World War II. During the war several conventional Nazi submarines had made use of the fringes of the pack as hiding places. After an attack on a convoy, they would dart under the edge of the ice, beyond reach of Allied anti-submarine vessels. However, these excursions were extremely brief and provided no scientific data not already developed by other sources.

After World War II, a scientist at the United States Naval Electronics Laboratory in San Diego, Dr. Waldo Lyon, a soft-spoken physicist whom I would soon come to know and admire, suggested that a United States submarine be included in an Arctic military exercise known as HIGHJUMP. Lyon's group at the San Diego laboratory had, since 1940, been studying the relationship of the submarine to its environment, the sea. Lyon was just plain curious to know what might happen when a submarine entered a frozen sea. The operation was carried out, and Lyon returned to San Diego tremendously interested in the Arctic. At his suggestion the name of his branch was changed to "Submarine and Arctic Research Division".

A year later, with Dr. Lyon aboard, a United States submarine, the Boarfish, steamed cautiously beneath the ice pack, penetrating to a distance of six miles. Afterwards Lyon developed an inverted fathometer, which could be used to bounce echoes upward off the ice, thus enabling the submarine to measure its distance below the ice. In 1948 this equipment was installed on the upper deck of the submarine Carp, and a limited run beneath the ice was conducted.

In the same year, meanwhile, interest in submarine operations beneath the ice pack had developed in a new quarter. Commander Robert D. McWethy, a submariner on duty as an instructor at a navigational school in Monterey, found one day that his schedule called for a week of lectures on Arctic navigation, about which he knew very little. McWethy had heard that the Air Force was experimenting with navigational techniques in the Arctic, so he wangled some time off and a ride across the Pole in an Air Force plane. He was astonished to see, from an altitude of 18,000 feet, leads and polynias in the ice. One of the Air Force men asked him:

"Why can't you people operate submarines up here?"

"I don't know," McWethy replied.

The idea had been born, and it soon became an all-consuming sideline with McWethy. By 1949 he had become so fascinated with the Arctic region that he persuaded the Navy's Bureau of Personnel to station him aboard an unlikely ship for a submariner, the ice-breaker Burton Island. Crashing through thick ice from one open stretch of water to the next, in the frozen wasteland off Alaska, McWethy, like Sir Hubert Wilkins, dreamed of a conventional submarine ducking beneath these barriers with ease. On all trips the Burton Island's fathometer pinged away steadily, charting a sea bottom that had never been thoroughly surveyed. The information she compiled would later serve us well.

In 1950 Dr. Lyon came aboard the Burton Island for a short research tour. Since both Lyon and McWethy were of like mind, it was not surprising that letters soon began to flow to the Chief of Naval Operations, pointing out the possibilities of the Arctic as a submarine manoeuvring area. Although there were many reservations, largely as a result of Dr. Lyon's suggestions in 1952, the submarine Redfish was ordered to make an ice-pack probe. Equipped with Dr. Lyon's gear, she penetrated beneath the pack a distance over twenty miles and remained submerged for eight hours. After that, however, top-level interest in polar operations for submarines began to wane.

But neither Lyon nor McWethy gave up. By late 1956 McWethy had gravitated to an important job on the staff of the Chief of Naval Operations. He was there when CNO received a letter from Senator Henry M. Jackson of Washington, who had just returned from an Arctic tour with the Air Force, asking if it would be feasible to operate a nuclear-powered submarine beneath the ice pack. CNO passed the letter to McWethy for a reply, which, of course, was an enthusiastic yes.

In theory, a nuclear-powered submarine was an ideal instrument with which to explore the Arctic. With her ability to go very deep, she could pass well beneath even the thickest ice one might expect to find in the Arctic. Since her nuclear engine required no air and would not become quickly exhausted as do conventional submarine batteries, she could remain submerged for an indefinite period, creeping as slowly, or speeding as swiftly, as she desired. She would not have to risk surfacing in leads or polynias unless she so desired. Warm and relaxed in a controlled environment, her crew would experience no physical discomfort. She could be equipped with a great variety of instruments to record the characteristics of the ice, the water, and the sea bottom.

In the process of answering Senator Jackson's letter, the Chief of Naval Operations, Admiral Burke, told his staff: "Let's really look into this." And thus it was, as I later learned, that I found myself camping between bookshelves of the main Navy library.

The gripping, dramatic stories of man's efforts to conquer the polar pack made good reading, but I was seeking information such as (1) how thick is the ice? (2) how deep is the water? and (3) do icebergs, with their deadly, deep keels drift through the pack? The scientific information available, including some published Russian sources, was conflicting, and confirmed—if confirmation is needed—that the Arctic is a virtually unexplored area. No two "authorities" seemed to agree on anything.

Even so, the longer I studied and let my mind dwell on the Arctic, the more enthusiastic I became about the possibility of a polar voyage, whatever form it might take. Initially, McWethy had proposed a north-west transit, up along the coast of Alaska, through McClure Strait and the Canadian Islands, the route to be blazed by the Coast Guard ships Spar, Bramble, and Storis in 1957. But this idea was instantly torpedoed. My own feeling was that nuclear submarine operations beneath the ice should begin where Sir Hubert Wilkins had made his ill-fated attempt, in the deep waters between Greenland and Spitsbergen. I envisaged a series of summer-time probes, each longer in length than the previous one, the whole operation to be stretched over a period of years.

Everyone I talked with seemed interested in the voyage, but I soon discovered that many of the men who count, the senior naval commanders, viewed even a very conservative approach as foolhardy. Their general comment was: "Why risk our only nuclear submarine in that unknown area?" One admiral told me in no uncertain terms, "That trip you are talking about will never happen. You might as well relax."

But once gripped with the polar bug, it is impossible to relax. By the spring of 1957, I, in my own small way, and McWethy, who briefed more than ten thousand officers, including thirty-five admirals, had begun to overwhelm the opposition. Actually, many factors worked in our favour. By then it was clear to strategic planners that when the nuclear-powered, missile-firing submarine became a reality, the Arctic, dominating over three thousand miles of Soviet coastline, would be an ideal launching spot. Conversely, there was a growing fear that the Russians, who no doubt are building nuclear-powered submarines of their own, might dominate the area for the same purpose. Then in the spring, the controversy moved on to the headquarters of Rear Admiral C. W. Wilkins, Commander, Submarines, Atlantic. A man of great vision and daring, he

became one of the strongest and most enthusiastic proponents
of the trip.

Finally in June 1957, after almost a full year in NRB under
Admiral Rickover, I left for the West Coast to take command
of the Nautilus. At that time I felt that an Arctic trip in the
summer of 1957 was a certainty, but I had yet to receive an
official green light.

FIVE

A Great Ship—An Extraordinary Crew

When I reached San Francisco, the proposed Arctic cruise was very much on my mind, but now I faced an immediate and not-so-simple problem: that of relieving Captain Wilkinson of command of Nautilus, of integrating myself into the crew and gaining their respect and confidence. This would be especially ticklish, since almost the minute I took command I would have to tell them of the contemplated polar trip.

Nautilus was at sea. Arrangements were made for me to join her by helicopter. I would ride the ship to Seattle and formally take command there.

As we thrashed out over the water, I felt no special sense of exhilaration. As a matter of fact, I spent most of the time wondering if the pilot had ever before manoeuvred over a weaving submarine deck. Then, below us, we could see the dark, sleek form of Nautilus, bobbing on the surface. Men were scampering around topside making preparations for the helicopter transfer. We eased down close to the deck and hovered. I descended the remaining distance in a sling. Wilkinson gave me a warm greeting. Shortly afterwards we submerged for the run to Seattle.

Much has been written of Nautilus' nuclear power plant and her performance record. After living aboard her for several days, two things impressed me almost as much as the plant. One was the crew, the other the comfort, or "habitability," as the technicians call it.

Nautilus is quite large as submarines go. She measures 320 feet from bow to stern, and 28 feet in diameter.

Since she does not carry a large battery nor a great volume of Diesel fuel, which on conventional submarines occupy nearly half the total space inside the hull, it is possible to devote considerably more room to living accommodation.

The Wardroom, for example, is nearly four times the size of the Wardroom on conventional submarines. The Crew's Mess is, relatively speaking, huge. Thirty-six men can be fed at one time, and in a matter of five minutes the Mess compartment can be converted to a movie theatre for fifty people. The Crew's Mess is also equipped with an ice-cream machine, a Coke machine, and a built-in hi-fi system, the core of which is a juke box that gives five plays for a nickel. In addition, Nautilus carries an automatic washer and dryer, a nucleonics laboratory, a complete machine shop, a photographic dark-room with enlarging facilities, and a library containing more than six hundred volumes. The appointments and colour scheme on Nautilus were conceived by one of America's leading decorators.

Many other items make for comfortable living. In the tile-decked washrooms there are individual small stainless-steel drawers for toilet articles. Each member of the crew has his own bunk with a comfortable foam-rubber mattress (on conventional fleet submarines sailors often share bunks, a practice known as "hot-bunking"), and each bunk is equipped with a shoe rack.

On long submerged runs a special piece of equipment which we call a "CO_2 scrubber" removes poisonous gases from the atmosphere; oxygen is bled into the ship as necessary from a large bank of bottles. Massive air-conditioning units maintain the temperature on Nautilus somewhere between 68 and 72 degrees, the relative humidity about 50 per cent. One Nautilus sailor, John P. McGovern, who has been aboard since the ship was commissioned, says, "We've been in the tropics, we've been far north, but the atmosphere inside Nautilus always remains the same. Even in the coldest waters, I've never worn a jacket on Nautilus."

Of all Nautilus' assets, the greatest, perhaps, is the crew. As I learned in a few days, this is no ordinary submarine crew.

These are the Olympic champions of submariners, the cream of the force. Hand-picked, carefully trained, averaging twenty-six years old (two-thirds of them are married), they are the finest and proudest submariners in the history of the Navy.

Before joining Nautilus, all officers and engineering ratings—regardless of past experience in submarines—study nuclear propulsion for a full year. The study consists of six months of academic work in the Nuclear Power School, New London, Connecticut, followed by six months of operational training on the Nautilus land-based prototype at Arco, Idaho. Nautilus herself serves as a kind of advanced training establishment. She has furnished nine officers and forty-four enlisted men who now man other nuclear submarines. A good indication of the level of intelligence and ability of the enlisted men can be got from this statistic: of the 288 crewmen who have served on Nautilus, forty-seven have been promoted to officer status or have entered programmes leading to commissions.

This is not to say that the men on the Nautilus are operational perfectionists. Like any other ship, company, or organization, she has had her share of mistakes. One time on a submerged endurance run from Key West to New London, she unknowingly sped into a trawler's fishnet. The captain of the trawler, as he later reported in the papers, was astonished when all at once he, his boat, and his nets, which had been crawling to the south, began speeding northward at over twenty knots. Under my command, during a naval manoeuvre in European waters, we picked up what we thought was a "heavy," or aircraft carrier, on our sonar. We made an approach by sonar and fired two practice torpedoes. The ship turned out to be an innocent British merchantman and I believe, perhaps because the Suez incident was then at its height, the captain of the merchantman was quite alarmed to see the torpedoes screaming down on him. I spent two days apologizing through official British channels for that one.

Nor are Nautilus sailors dull, hard-working, nuclear bookworms. On the contrary, they are as spirited and carefree as the usual submarine crew—perhaps more so.

An example, which I heard about soon after reporting on board, was the case of a very bright hospital corpsman, whose name I will omit for reasons that will become apparent shortly.

Nautilus is a widely travelled ship. Since her commissioning she has steamed well over 130,000 miles and called at scores of ports in the United States, Europe, and the Caribbean area.

At these various ports the hospital corpsman in question went ashore, not in Navy uniform but in civilian clothes. So dressed, he cut quite a figure—a handsome drake, with plenty of savoir-faire. He would always head directly for the finest hotels and night clubs, and very shortly establish his identity as Major Keating of the Royal Algerian Balloon Corps. His shipmates, who always went along with the gag, were briefed to drop occasional confirmatory facts and information in the right ears, and soon Major Keating would accumulate an impressive number of social invitations and free drinks—his major objective, of course.

Once when Nautilus stopped in Bermuda, Major Keating overnight became a smashing success. As each day passed, he gravitated into higher social circles, attending party after party in his honour. With Nautilus' departure time drawing close, Major Keating, the perfect gentleman, arranged his own party to return the hospitality. He laid on a dinner party at one of the fanciest hotels, issuing invitations to about two dozen people. After giving the place, he added, "Please come about six o'clock. I may be a bit late—I have some pressing affairs to attend to—but please go right ahead. Don't let them delay the refreshments or dinner. I will join you later."

That day Nautilus sailed at 4:00 P.M. and Major Keating, at sea, had returned to his true identity as a hospital corpsman. His guests arrived at the hotel at six, and presumably had a lively evening, in spite of the fact that Major Keating failed to appear. No doubt they were astonished when they found, again, that they had been stuck with the bill.

Since her commissioning, Nautilus has been a kind of floating exhibit of practical nuclear power and, not surprisingly, many dignitaries have come on board to see her in action. No less than 68 members of Congress, 186 admirals, and various Secretaries of the Navy and of the Defence Department have signed her logbook.

When Admiral Robert B. Carney was Chief of Naval Operations, he came on board for a brief visit. During a slack period he was sitting in the Wardroom with a couple of the ship's officers, including Lieutenant Ken Carr, who asked if the Admiral would sign the logbook. The Admiral replied that he would be delighted but he hadn't a pen. Carr offered his. Admiral Carney, writing with his left hand, began scratching his name in the book but, alas, the pen leaked, making a tremendous splotch.

"This is the worst pen I have ever seen," said Admiral Carney.

Carr, who felt very proud of Nautilus and everything on board, including the fountain pens, piped back: "Well, Admiral, you know you're the first left-handed Chief of Naval Operations we've ever had aboard."

When dignitaries come on board, we usually give them a turn at the ship's controls—the bow planes, the stern planes, and the rudder control, or helm. This gives them a good feel of the ship and its amazing manoeuvrability. On one occasion we had aboard an unusual cluster of admirals. A four-star admiral manned the stern planes, a three-star admiral the bow planes, and a two-star admiral the helm.

Just at that moment, a Nautilus seaman, who normally stood his watches on the planes and helm, came walking into the compartment. He took one look at all that gold braid and, in a voice just loud enough to be heard, cracked, "By golly, they always put the junior man on the helm."

An interesting Wardroom character, I soon learned, was Lieutenant Commander Paul Early, the Chief Engineer. Few men know the operation of nuclear reactors as well as he, but Early could rank with the original Malaprop. He mixes up every cliché and adage. On the Nautilus, his malapropisms have come to be called "Earlyisms". Some examples that come to mind: "That guy's a two-flusher"; "That's just water under

D

the dam"; "Stop pushing my leg"; "That story dog-tails right
into this"; "The fitting is tight as a fiddle."

I believe a free press reflects the spirit, the concern, the
weakness, and foibles of the group of society under its scrutiny.
On board Nautilus we have our own press, a newspaper which
is published almost every day. In many ways the paper is
unique. First, it is considered Top Secret, one reason being
that if the material printed in this paper were to be published
elsewhere it would be libellous. Secondly, the paper, which is
put out by a lively and outspoken character named John H.
Michaud, changes its name every day, in keeping with fast-
moving Nautilus, a ship that does not stay put in one place
very long. It usually carries a cartoon by Nautilus' talented
William J. McNally, Jr., who is also a magician, a hypnotist,
and master of ceremonies at most of our parties.

Often the paper has this notation: "Contributions for this
sheet are accepted from all hands. No words barred. Do your
damnedest. No secrets—we tell all—if you see your name
today, use your 'friends's' tomorrow."

Some samples of titbits, a few that can be quoted without
engendering a libel suit:

> Latest "sack time" study by the Executive Officer has our
> Gunnery Department head logging 19 hours a day, even with the
> time changes.

> *Wanted*—Information on why Lt. Boyd is aboard. Anyone
> having information kindly inform Lt. Boyd.

> *Quote of the day:* "Last week I didn't even know how to spell
> Ensign, next week I'll be one."

> *Can You Beat This:* McCoole is going all out this trip. His
> record so far is: Has not missed a meal since San Francisco.
> Logged a minimum of 16 hours per day sack time (to maintain
> third place in the Chief Petty Officer sack time tournament),
> and his goal is to be the fattest ensign ever commissioned.

One day the paper contained this item:

> At press time, and with no articles in the action basket, it

appears that most of the "dirt" aboard has been cleaned up. But like all good newspapers we have our "ace in the hole". Unless more articles are submitted, and as a last recourse, we shall go to the service records of a select group and publish the facts as forwarded to us from the FBI, Panama Law Enforcement Group, San Diego cops, and San Francisco Police Release Division. As only a few know, we did have a number of releases there.

The Nautilus newspaper is indeed a free press. No one is spared, not even the Captain.

As we sped submerged toward Seattle, the more I saw of this crew, the more I realized that I was just about the luckiest guy in the world to have been chosen to command Nautilus. The crewmen were not only competent and spirited, but eager to exploit Nautilus' full capabilities, to write the book for nuclear submarine operations. They were proud of the ship's firsts. And there were many of them.

An example, and likewise an example of Nautilus' daring, was our approach into Seattle. Puget Sound was crawling with small boats, pleasure craft around which it is sometimes difficult to manoeuvre in a narrow channel. The water was quite deep, so Captain Wilkinson said, "We can get in a lot faster by steaming beneath them."

Fully submerged, passing beneath sailboats and power-boats, Nautilus threaded through the winding channel with only her periscope exposed. When we were almost directly alongside the pier where we were scheduled to moor, Wilkinson, manning the periscope, gave the word to surface. We came up vertically; a few moments later the lines were secure.

Seldom in my days of submarining had I seen anything to equal that manoeuvre. Needless to say, by the time I took formal command of the ship from Wilkinson, I was no longer concerned about the crew's reaction to a probe beneath the polar ice pack. I was certain that if the crew developed confidence in me, they would take Nautilus anywhere any time.

SIX

Final Preparations

From the point of view of most of the top naval personnel, Nautilus' number one mission in the months ahead was a NATO naval exercise, STRIKEBACK, to be conducted in European waters in late September. It would be the largest peacetime NATO naval manoeuvre in history, and all hands were eager to see how Nautilus could perform. All of us on Nautilus were looking forward to this exercise, but I must confess that at the time I took command of Nautilus my immediate thoughts were on the polar probe.

I was becoming increasingly concerned. The summer weeks were slipping rapidly past, and there was still no definite word that we would make the trip. In fact, when we arrived in San Diego in July to exercise with surface fleet units, I heard a rumour that the trip had been cancelled. I immediately got on the telephone with my boss in New London, Captain Thomas Henry, to ask if the trip was still a possibility.

To my relief he replied, "It is not only a possibility. It looks as if it is going to go through for sure."

Time was closing in. We had been ordered to arrive in England for STRIKEBACK on or about September 20. According to our timetable, which left no room for possible delays, that would allow us only ten days to spend at the ice pack. Worse was the fact that we would be arriving at the edge of the pack relatively late in the year, in the latter part of August, when the weather is not ideal and the ice begins to rebuild for the winter.

I looked up Dr. Waldo Lyon at the Naval Electronics Laboratory in San Diego. When I told him that the ice probe

was certain to go through, he, better than most, recognized
the need for haste.

He and I held lengthy conferences, during which we at
first discussed the scope of the operation. From his previous
experiences under the ice on Boarfish, Carp, and Redfish,
Dr. Lyon was convinced that Nautilus could safely make a
fairly deep and extensive penetration. We did not discuss
going to the North Pole. The main objective, as we saw it, was
to cover a lot of territory and learn as much as possible in the
limited time allotted to the probe. Our views were put in a letter
which we mailed off to New London and Washington.

I then suggested to Dr. Lyon that we might save time by
loading on board Nautilus most of his special upward-scanning
fathometers, or ice detectors, then and there. He agreed, and
offered to send two men to New London to meet us on our
arrival, and proceed without delay with installation of the
gear. Meanwhile, I asked Washington to have a man from the
Hydrographic Office meet us in Panama with all the latest
Arctic charts, soundings, ice reports, and whatever other
information was available. By the time we reached New
London on July 21, we had studied all these data, and Dr.
Lyon's men were waiting on the dock to begin work.

I learned on reaching New London that during our trip
from Panama to the East Coast, the polar trip had very nearly
been cancelled. But when I checked with Captain Henry, he
said, "There is only one man now who can stop the cruise."

"Who is that?" I asked.

"You," he said.

"Well, it certainly will not be me," I replied.

Commander McWethy had been transferred up from
Washington, Dr. Lyon arrived from San Diego, and very soon
we were all engaged in high-level conferences with Commander
Submarines, Atlantic, Rear Admiral Wilkins. During one of
these conferences, final plans were made for an event I had
suggested several months previously: an aerial reconnaissance
of the ice under which we intended to operate.

On August 5 a small party—consisting of myself and my

Navigator, Lieutenant Bill Lalor, Commander McWethy, Dr. Lyon, and Commander Les Kelly, skipper of the conventional submarine Trigger, which was scheduled to accompany us on the polar probe as a "buddy ship," and others—climbed aboard a Navy Super-Constellation radar warning plane and flew north. We landed at Thule Air Force Base, Greenland, to refuel and catch some sleep. During the stop-over in Thule, all submarine officers removed their dolphins to forestall some Air Force type from asking, "What are all you submariners doing up here?" Our polar probe was a classified exercise.

Next morning, August 6, we took off and again headed north, skimming along barely six hundred feet above the ice. It looked cold and rugged, and I marvelled at the thought of men setting out across that wilderness on sledges. The ice reminded me of some huge jigsaw puzzle. In some areas it was fitted together perfectly, seemingly forming a solid layer, the joints barely perceptible to the eye. In other places the pieces of the puzzle had yet to be laid in place. It was a helter-skelter mess of floes, blocks, and chunks, drifting around in open stretches of water. However, there was far less open water than I had been led to believe. Throughout the trip I remained glued to a window, with a movie camera trained on the ice. After flying nearly a thousand miles over our proposed track, we headed south and landed in Iceland. Next day we flew home.

I found Nautilus, berthed at the Electric Boat Company, swarming with workmen wielding welding torches and other tools. The installation of Dr. Lyon's five inverted fathometers was going well. Other repair jobs on Nautilus' regular machinery were progressing satisfactorily.

From an equipment standpoint, I then turned my attention to our compasses, which, by all odds, would be the most critical item once we slid beneath the ice.

At that time Nautilus was equipped with two types of compass, one magnetic and one gyro, plus an auxiliary, or stand-by, gyro. Almost everyone at some time in his life has come into contact with a magnetic compass. I have seen them mounted in automobiles, on bicycles, and carried in the knapsacks of boy scouts. They are very simple in principle. The needle, influenced by the earth's magnetic field, points north. If they are mounted near or upon metal, as in an automobile, adjustments must be made for local interference, called "deviation".

A magnetic compass, however, does not actually point to true north, or the geographic North Pole. A magnetic compass points toward a hypothetical position known as the Magnetic Pole, which is several hundred miles south of the true Pole. Thus, depending on one's position on the earth, allowances for this displacement must be made. These corrections are called "variation," and they are usually plotted on charts. Assuming all corrections for local deviation have been made, a sailor on a boat in Long Island Sound, using only a magnetic compass and seeking to steer a true northerly course, might actually steer several degrees away from north as indicated on his magnetic compass.

A modern gyrocompass, on the other hand, is a complex piece of mechanics and electronics, based on the principle of the gyroscope (its main insides whirl, say, at about 22,000 revolutions per minute), and if it is operating properly in non-extreme latitudes, it always points toward true north, or the geographic North Pole. Under ordinary circumstances, no correction for local influences, or deviation, is required, nor is it necessary to apply the variation factor. All the major ships of the United States Navy and many merchantmen are equipped with gyrocompasses.

In the case of both the magnetic compasses and gyrocompasses, the farther one moves north, the less reliable they become. When it comes within a thousand miles of the Magnetic Pole, the magnetic compass becomes confused, and the needle is apt to swing wildly, or walk around in complete circles. Similarly, the gyrocompass, as it approaches the true geographic pole, loses its stability, for reasons that are much too complex to explain here.

Under the ice, following a virtually uncharted ocean bottom, if the compasses went haywire, a submarine, with no other reference points, could get into serious trouble.

For example, take Submarine X. Fitted with conventional compasses, it ducks under the ice in the area between Greenland and Spitsbergen, proceeding due north. As it moves toward the Pole, the gyrocompass starts to drift slowly, undetectably, to the right, due to a faulty electronic amplifier and the virtually nil north directional force encountered near 90 degrees north latitude. Next, the magnetic compass becomes almost useless because the Magnetic Pole is too close. Unknown currents push Submarine X farther to the right. As the Pole is approached, the gyrocompass drift reverses itself, causing the submarine unknowingly to make a slow circle around the Pole. Errors compound with amazing rapidity and Submarine X ends up heading, perhaps, toward a landlocked coastline, or who knows where, all the time without the slightest indication that she is a victim of "longitude roulette," as we call it on the Nautilus.

In investigating these problems, I heard that the Gyroscope Company had designed a new compass, called the Mark 19, that was vastly more efficient in high latitudes. En route from Panama to New London, I radioed a request for one of these compasses and during our short period of preparation in New London, the Mark 19 was installed and the crew instructed in its maintenance.

Satisfied that with the installation of the Mark 19 we had done all we could with respect to the under-ice navigation problem, we next turned our minds to the other hazards we might encounter, such as fire, or the breakdown of some critical piece of machinery that would completely immobilize us under the ice pack. Every man inspected and re-inspected his equipment. Paul Early and a group of men made a gimlet-eye tour of the ship checking for possible fire hazards. They combed everything from fuse-box connections with the nuclear power plant to the electric toasters in the galley.

Although my knowledge of the ice conditions was far from perfect, I was certain that even if we became hopelessly lost or if disaster loomed on board Nautilus, we could always reach the surface. If we were not able to locate a lead or polynia, we could tilt the ship up at an angle and fire a salvo of six torpedoes into the underside of the ice. If that didn't open a hole, we still had nineteen more torpedoes to send behind them. If we couldn't force the entire ship through the hole, we could at least push up the sail—the streamlined housing for our periscopes, radar, and radio antennae. Thus we could make radio contact with the outside world and request aid— spare parts or whatever was necessary to repair the damage on Nautilus—to be air-dropped to us. We could even completely abandon ship, if necessary, since there is a hatch leading up to the bridge on the sail.

Against the remote possibility of a dire emergency of this kind, we loaded on board Nautilus a large supply of cold-weather clothing, including parkas, heavy shoes, heavy socks, thick Army trousers, Army shirts, heavy Navy jackets and knitted helmets, and sweaters. Nautilus was becoming crowded: along with this, the men had stored away a ninety-day supply of food, which would last us through the polar probe and Exercise STRIKEBACK.

The conventional submarine Trigger, much slower than Nautilus, got under way several days in advance, so that she would be on station at the outer edge of the pack by the time we arrived. For Nautilus there was one final operational question I wanted to clear. My orders from Admiral Wilkins, which had been drafted by his staff, read: "At discretion proceed under the ice to the vicinity of 83 degrees north latitude and return." 83 degrees north latitude is about 420 miles from the North Pole, 240 miles north of the edge of the ice pack.

I asked my boss, Captain Henry, "Do you have any comments on how I should interpret 'vicinity'? In other words, could I go to the North Pole?"

"We have confidence in the Nautilus to do the right thing," he replied. "We know you'll use the proper interpretation."

Thus the question of actually going all the way to the North Pole on this first probe was left entirely up to me. Naturally, I secretly hoped that we could. However, I was never certain that we could make it. It would depend on many circumstances

—how the crew, including me, fared beneath the ice and how the compasses performed. As far as our scientific mission was concerned, going to the Pole was a desirable but not a critical objective.

At the eleventh hour in our preparations an event occurred which deeply distressed all of us on Nautilus. Admiral Wilkins suffered a heart attack, and was rushed to the Naval Hospital in Portsmouth, Virginia. Four days before we departed and only two or three days after he arrived at the hospital, he wrote me a letter, in which he said:

> I want to wish you and your people every success in the cruise ahead. There are those who look on this operation askance and with scepticism. I am not one of those. I believe it is a venture of great promise, in both the fields of national defence and science. I am sure the information you will collect will be of great value. The operation itself is one that appeals to the imagination and the venturesome spirit within men's souls. You will be pioneers and trail blazers. Your findings may lead the way to under-ice navigational capabilities for nuclear-powered submarines that may make it possible for them to go any place in the ice regions where the interest of national defence requires. I know you have done careful planning for this operation, that all foreseen hazards have been taken into careful account, and that every possible preparation has been made to ensure a successful operation, which will add to Nautilus' laurels and the glories achieved by her officers and men.

Following the receipt of that encouraging letter from Admiral Wilkins, we on Nautilus bid our families farewell, and at 0800 on August 19, 1957, backed away from our slip. Destination: edge of the ice pack between Greenland and Spitsbergen, and afterwards an unparalleled adventure.

SEVEN

The Journey North

We cleared the shallow waters of Block Island Sound and, later, the hundred-fathom curve. Then we took Nautilus under for a trim dive—to get the ship in proper balance.

As usual after a relatively long period alongside a dock we found a discouraging number of minor deficiencies. The diver's light, a powerful lamp we had mounted topside so that we could illuminate the underside of the ice for periscope observation, flooded out. The bathythermograph, an instrument we use to measure the temperature of the sea water, went out of commission. Number one periscope had been badly packed. It was difficult to train, and a maddening trickle of salt water ran down the back of my neck.

"A hundred-million-dollar home and the roof leaks," said a crewman.

It is strange how a remark of that kind will conjure up the past. As I pushed and strained at the balky periscope, watching the grey, rolling seas through the cross hairs, my mind wandered back to 1946.

The war was over then, and for the first time Bonny, our baby Mike, and I had an opportunity to settle down as a family. In New London, where I had come to help mothball our ship, the Trutta, it was not easy to find housing. We rented a home out near Black Point Beach, for about $100 a month. About May, a real-estate agent sent some people around to look at the house. We thought this very odd because we had no intention of moving. I asked the agent what it was all about and he replied, "Well, I figured you folks wouldn't want to stay on past June because in that month the rent goes up to four hundred dollars a month." When we took the house, we didn't realize—had not been informed, in fact—that in the summer season beach homes were sky-high, much too high for a lieutenant's salary. We had to get out.

I was infuriated, and I made up my mind then and there that I would never again place myself at the mercy of a landlord. I would build my own house.

Everyone thought I was slightly daft. Building materials were scarce or non-existent. There was no new construction under way in the New London area. Nevertheless, I scrounged here and there, hired a couple of carpenters, and in late afternoons and weekends started the house. I was thankful then for my boyhood experience in the lumber mill and woodshop. I can honestly say that I built about 50 per cent of the house myself. People came around just out of curiosity to see this "young fool" trying to put up a house. They predicted that I would never be able to get roofing materials. If I did, the roof would surely leak because its slope was much less than that of a traditional New England house! It was an impossible goal.

Well, the house was built, and we lived in it for a long time, and the roof did not leak. The impossible project had proved feasible. *Now*, I thought, as I lowered the periscope, *here is Anderson embarked on another "impossible" project. I wonder if we will be as successful.*

The senior officers of Nautilus had turned their attention to one final item which, because of the pressure and confusion in port, we had not yet got round to: indoctrination of the crew in under-ice operations. Although the exercise was technically classified, every man aboard knew where we were headed. When word of exactly what we proposed to do on the expedition got around, our ship's physician, Dr. R. F. Dobbins, reported that 90 per cent of the men were "somewhat apprehensive".

To dispel this apprehension, my Executive Officer on this voyage, Lieutenant Commander Warren R. Cobean, planned a prolonged series of lectures on the Arctic and the ice pack.

Accompanying these lectures, he showed movies in the Crew's Mess, some of which I had taken during the aerial reconnaissance in the Navy Super-Constellation. After the first showing of the movies, one Nautilus sailor remarked, "Ice. Ice. Ice. Nothing but ice. Boy, I'll tell you it's going to be a drunk night when we reach England."

We surfaced that first evening to work on the leaky periscope. While this work was in progress, a naval vessel passed us close abeam and, as is customary, challenged us by searchlight. We replied, giving our identification, and he came back: "Where bound?" I considered replying "North Pole," and although, in a sense, it was almost the truth, I thought he might consider it flippant. So instead we replied that we were bound for a classified mission.

At last the leak in the periscope was stopped, and we slid beneath the waves into our true medium, setting a northward course at high speed. Life on Nautilus returned to routine, broken only by one special drill: a vertical, elevator-like ascent, which we would have to know how to do if we surfaced through a crack or patch of water in the ice. (Ordinarily, submarines surface with forward momentum.) I spent my time studying the little information available to us on the pack, or playing poker with the officers in the Wardroom. Back in the stern Crew Quarters, one Nautilus sailor, John Hargraves, was building a very intricate model of a sailing ship. When he left it unattended, he attached a sign to it: "I know it's put together wrong and will break, but let me foul it up myself."

Our daily newspaper came on the "stands". The issue of Friday, August 23, labelled "Top Secret," ran a cartoon showing the famous Major Keating of the Royal Algerian Balloon Corps, decked out in explorer's regalia, including heavy winter clothing, standing in the forward Torpedo Room. The caption explained that Major Keating had set out to find the shortest route from bow to stern of the Nautilus. On that same day, I overheard two of the Stewards talking about going under the ice. One, James Owens, said that he had a fair amount of faith in the skipper to do the right thing. The other, Donald

Wilson, replied, "I have, too. But I'd still rather be in New London."

One problem for some men on the Nautilus, and a fairly serious one at that, is a constant inclination toward obesity. The food we serve is the best in the Navy, and the men eat heartily. At the same time, confined as they are, they have little opportunity to work it off physically. On this trip, we had brought along bathroom scales for the Wardroom, and everyone was naturally quite weight-conscious.

This concern inspired the younger officers to play an ingenious joke on Dr. Dobbins, who was spearheading the anti-obesity movement. Every morning, when Doc Dobbins was off watch and asleep, one of the officers would slip into his stateroom and cut an eighth-inch piece from his khaki-webbed belt. As the days passed, of course, it became more and more difficult for Dr. Dobbins to get his belt buckle to connect and, we supposed, he believed his waist was getting larger and larger. After four or five days, we noted, he began to pass up his desserts. We let him go on like this, penalizing himself unnecessarily, for many days before we let him in on the secret.

By Tuesday, August 27, we were fairly far north—in the vicinity of Iceland. I thought it was time to give the crew a little added reassurance, so over the public address system I said:

"Men. This is the Captain. This is going to be one hell of an interesting cruise from now on, particularly starting about Saturday. I hope there is no one on board who thinks it will be grim or in any way unsafe. If I thought for one moment we might even halfway jeopardize this magnificent ship, or her magnificent crew, I would turn around and head for port right now."

Later, my Executive Officer reported that whatever apprehension had existed on leaving New London was now completely gone. "Captain, they are as ready as anyone could ever be. They will go anywhere with you."

By Wednesday, August 28, we were cruising deep in little-travelled waters, and I cautioned the duty officers to maintain constant vigilance, especially for underwater obstacles, such as an uncharted peak in the ocean bottom, or an unreported iceberg. About one o'clock that morning, while I was sound asleep, I felt the ship heel violently with a terrific up-angle. Cups, saucers, ash trays, and other loose gear crashed to the deck. I leaped from my bunk and ran to the control room.

The Conning Officer reported: "Solid sonar contact nine hundred yards dead ahead." He had thrown fast-moving Nautilus into the manoeuvre to avoid it. As more sonar information came in on the contact, we soon realized that it was a very large fish, perhaps a shark or a whale. I commended the Conning Officer for taking the proper evasive action, and, confident that the crew was tuned to perfect pitch, I returned to my bunk and slept soundly the remainder of the night.

On Thursday we went very deep and opened Nautilus wide, as a kind of ceremony in honour of our crossing the Arctic Circle. A few minutes later we came to periscope depth to check the weather. It was typically Arctic: solid overcast, heavy fog, visibility about three hundred yards. Next day off Jan Mayen Island, we slowed and got on the underwater telephone, which has a range of about seven miles, to make contact with Trigger. She was waiting at the pre-arranged rendezvous point. As a joke, the first order I gave Les Kelly was: "Request you head for the North Pole." Les is a keen-minded officer. He immediately came back: "What speed?"

While the crew was operating as a perfect team, Nautilus was, from a technical standpoint, far from her peak condition. The number one periscope was still hard to train, and other minor machinery was reported out of commission. Of greater concern to me was the CO_2 scrubber, the machine that keeps the poisonous gases below harmful levels inside the boat. It had been temperamental since leaving New London, and in spite of constant repairs it was still not functioning efficiently. However, we were determined to push on.

South of the pack we surfaced, after steaming over four thousand miles in eleven days beneath the surface, the longest submerged run on Nautilus up to that time. We transferred to

Trigger some cold-weather clothing and other gear that had arrived after her departure. Then, still on the surface, we continued north. Trigger was not equipped with the new Mark 19 gyrocompass, and already her old-fashioned gyrocompass had become erratic. Thankful for the Mark 19, we gave Trigger several course checks.

A small chunk of drift ice passed to starboard, another to port. From the bridge of Nautilus I gave the order to slow the great nuclear-driven propellers, and the ship coasted quietly in the cold water. At long last we had arrived at the edge of the unknown, the ice pack. It lay before us, stretching seemingly unbroken to the horizon, a trackless, colourless desert, highlighted by a kind of bright halo, a phenomenon known to men of the North as iceblink.

A gentle breeze cuffed the water; patches of fog drifted by. It was fairly comfortable on the bridge, not much colder than Long Island Sound in January. As I stared in fascination at that inhospitable blanket of ice, I recalled the mysteries, tragedies, and terrible physical discomforts which had occurred there as man, striving for the uncommon experience, had matched his comparatively small energies and resources against this gigantic physical barrier. The names rushed to mind: Ross, Peary, Cook, Amundsen, Stefansson, Wilkins. To know that we on the Nautilus would soon be steaming beneath the ice pack—crossing, as it were, under their footprints—filled us with a sense of history and a calculated respect for this barren wilderness.

Alongside us, her Diesels throbbing, and emitting white smoke as the warm exhaust met the nippy Arctic, lay Trigger. According to the operation plan, she would remain outside the pack during our penetrations, to assist in gathering data on underwater sonar transmissions and, frankly, to furnish moral support.

I relayed word to Les Kelly that our first excursion under the ice would be brief—not over 150 miles—and that we would rendezvous with Trigger outside the pack approximately twenty hours after we dived. Later, after we had become

Chief Petty Officers' sleeping quarters.

One of the ship's cooks preparing turkey in the galley.

Nautilus surfacing. The sailor in the galley has to lean forward to keep his balance during the steep ascent.

familiar with conditions under the ice, and proficient in the use of our special ice-detecting equipment, and had checked our compass behaviour, we planned a major journey.

I informed the Conning Officer, Lieutenant Steven A. White, that he could clear the bridge and dive when ready. At exactly 2000, September 1, 1957, one hour and twenty-three minutes after we had arrived at the pack, the rasping "A-uuuu-guh, A-uuuu-guh" of the ship's diving klaxon reverberated throughout the compartments, and Nautilus nosed under.

I thought of relaying by underwater telephone some kind of earth-shaking message to Les Kelly on Trigger, but since history is so easily made both in the Arctic and on Nautilus, it seemed inappropriate. Uncertain of the thickness of the ice, we descended to several hundred feet, set a course due north, and, several minutes later, moving at a very slow speed, Nautilus passed far beneath the edge of the ice pack. In the Crew's Mess the last watch section was eating a routine dinner. In the background I could hear strains of Pat Boone's "Love Letters in the Sand," one of a hundred records on our juke box.

This, I thought, is the way to explore the Arctic!

E

EIGHT

Probing the Unknown

We steamed northward, plunging deeper into the unknown. Within a very short time Dr. Lyon's sonar equipment told us enough to form a good picture of the overhead ice, or so we thought at the time. Generally, we found, the Arctic ice pack is a huge, ever-moving mass, diverse in character. In places it consists only of small blocks and brash—which the crew quickly dubbed "B and B"—easily penetrable by any surface ship. (Brash is broken fragments of ice.) The great bulk of the ice, however, is made up of irregular floes, ranging in size from a few feet to ten or fifteen feet, but seldom more. The underside of the ice is not smooth, as many have believed, but distinctly irregular. The ice is laced with many leads and polynias, although those large enough to accommodate a submarine are far between, and certainly not frequent enough to permit a conventional submarine to puddle-jump, as Sir Hubert Wilkins had planned.

We did not know it at the time, but we were later to discover that Dr. Lyon's equipment, while collecting a mountain of fine data, was not giving us a complete picture of the ice or, more accurately, we were ignoring a very significant indication on the instruments.

Each instrument had two recording pens. One was rigged so that it obtained information from our depth gauge, which precisely indicated the surface water level, or the theoretical surface water level. (When we crossed occasional patches of open water, we verified its accuracy.) This pen drew one line on an ever-moving piece of paper. The second pen was connected directly to Dr. Lyon's upward-scanning fatho-

meter, and graphically drew a picture of the underside of
the ice, immediately below, and in precise relationship to,
the water level line. Thus as we moved along, the two pens,
in effect, traced a profile of the shape and thickness of the
ice.

What we did not know then, and would not find out until
our next polar voyage, was that the cyclic rate of Dr. Lyon's
upward-scanning fathometer was too slow for Nautilus' speed.
In other words, we were not sending signals to bounce against
the bottom of the ice and return at a rate fast enough to profile
the ice accurately. The result was that we were only getting
a partial picture. We noticed, for example, that we would
get an occasional dip in the pen, indicating the ice was,
perhaps, fifty or more feet thick. We dismissed these dips
as "ghosts," or imperfect returns from the sonar. In actuality,
they were not ghosts. They were deep-hanging pressure ridges,
dangerous and deadly to our operation. In other words, the
ice was much thicker, the pressure ridges much deeper, than
we thought.

After we had become adjusted to the sensation of cruising in
our silent, frigid world, I felt I would like to take a first-hand
look at the ice, so I ordered the ship brought up slowly and
raised the periscope. The water was greyish and not at all
dark, as the sunlight filtered through the ice. The floodlight we
had mounted topside was unnecessary. I turned the field of the
periscope up, bringing my eye, through magnification, within
a few feet of the underside of the floes, which appeared to be
scudding overhead like grey clouds. It was a fascinating but
eerie experience. In fact, it was a little unnerving. Since there
was nothing from a scientific standpoint to be gained by this,
I put the scope back down and tactfully suggested that the
curious find something else to do. It was much better watching
the ice on sonar.

We soon reached the turn-around point for our first excursion.
Shortly afterwards, the overhead sonar outlined a lead or
polynia that appeared to be unusually large. Since part of our
mission called for surfacing tactics, I decided we might as well

try it then. I felt confident that the crew could handle a vertical ascent with ease.

As we saw the picture on the sonar, there was not much room to spare—it was going to be something like threading a needle—but guided by the sonar picture, we were able to manoeuvre Nautilus directly beneath the hole. Then slowly—very slowly—we began to inch our way up. I raised the periscope to confirm the sonar readings. Everything seemed to be checking perfectly. I kept my eye glued into the periscope, expecting the upper glass to break water at any moment.

A split second later I was startled to find not water overhead, but solid ice! I thought it must be a very thin sheet—so thin that it had not registered on our sonar—and since there was nothing to do now to stop Nautilus' ascent, I waited for the periscope to shatter through the ice.

Instead, our vertical ascent terminated abruptly and a shudder swept through the ship. At that same instant everything went black inside the periscope. It was a baffling sensation, I called out: "Flood negative!" a command to fill our buoyancy control tank, which would take us down again.

Some of that old dispelled apprehension must have returned then, for the officers and men looked at me expectantly. All I could think of to say was:

"Number two periscope has had it."

Why it had happened, or even what had happened, I didn't know just then. Later, after a conference with Dr. Lyon, we determined that we had collided with a small block of ice adrift in the polynia. Unluckily for us it had struck the most sensitive spot on the submarine. I hoped my estimate of the damage had been pessimistic, and that the periscope glass might easily be repaired after we reached open water.

Recalling the old adage that after a fall it is better to get up and ride again immediately, I asked Dr. Lyon to signal when we reached another large polynia. Soon we were trying to thread the needle again, manoeuvring Nautilus beneath the opening.

We came up slowly and when we were directly in line, I raised number one periscope. Like number two, it was completely black! I immediately cancelled the surfacing attempt and ordered the ship to steam back to the edge of the ice pack and rendezvous with Trigger. At 1400 we made contact by underwater telephone, and an hour later emerged from the ice and surfaced. Our pit log showed that we had travelled 150 miles beneath the ice. We had achieved a record, but for the first time our magnificent ship had been wounded.

A quick topside inspection revealed that my estimate had not been over-pessimistic. The number two periscope was damaged beyond repair, and number one was badly bent. For a nuclear submarine with advanced sonar like Nautilus', a periscope is a helpful but not absolutely vital piece of equipment for under-ice excursions. However, a periscope is important in attacking an enemy ship. We would need a periscope for STRIKEBACK. And no time had been allowed in the schedule for major repairs. What this meant, then, was that in order to get ready for the manoeuvre, we would have to cancel ice operations and depart immediately for England. Needless to say, after our weeks of frenzied preparations this was a very disheartening turn of events. Of greater importance to me and the crew was that it meant Nautilus for the first time had failed in an assigned mission.

While I brooded over these facts, some of the technicians on board had gone topside to inspect the damage. Not long afterwards, Paul Early reported to me:

"Captain, there's a chance—a slight chance—that number one periscope might be bent back into its normal position."

I regarded this suggestion with great scepticism. Such an operation had never been done, even in a periscope repair shop, I was sure, much less at sea on the pitching, confined bridge of a submarine. To make matters worse a gale had blown up and a heavy sea was running. However, there was nothing to be lost in the attempt, so I gave my permission.

The work on that periscope is a stirring sea story in itself. Climbing into the howling wind, John Krawczyk, Robert

Scott, and John McGovern lugged several hydraulic jacks to the bridge. The jacks were wedged between the bent periscope and the aluminium superstructure of the sail. Then—very gently—they pumped the jacks, applying pressure against the periscope. The strong, stainless-steel barrel remained rigid. The aluminium backstop bent. Undaunted, the three men searched for a stronger backstop. After hours of experimenting, they worked out an ingenious system of cross-bracing.

Now, once again, they were ready to apply pressure to the jacks. Again, gently, the jack expanded. The bracing held, and little by little the barrel bent toward the vertical. Then, above the roar of the wind, the sailors heard an unfamiliar noise, a brittle snap. They examined the scope. Two feet down from the periscope glass they discovered that the barrel had split open. The dry nitrogen gas, which is maintained inside the periscope to prevent optical fogging, hissed out into the gale.

When I received word that the barrel had cracked—there was a gap in it about four inches long—I was ready to give up immediately. But Early asked for more time. "I'd like to try to get the welders to fill it in, Captain."

Even under ideal shop conditions, stainless-steel welding is a precise and exacting art. The heat of the torch must be kept low, and in proper balance, to deposit the molten metal. The men would not be able to use a back-up plate, because it was impossible to get down inside the periscope barrel. It really seemed incredible to me that Early would even propose a try at it, especially with the temperature near freezing and a thirty-to-forty knot gale lashing the bridge. But I guess at that point I didn't fully know the strength and depth of determination of the typical Nautilus sailor.

Stainless-steel welders are rare, actually, but we carried two on board, Richard T. Bearden and John B. Kurrus, to effect repairs on the reactor, which has many stainless-steel parts. Bearden and Kurrus got their gear together, allowing there was a chance—maybe only one in ten—that they could do the job.

When they reached the bridge, the wind was so strong that

it ripped their welding masks from their faces. To keep out the wind and cold, they rigged a tarpaulin over the working area. Beneath this tarpaulin, Bearden and Kurrus began work, stopping every few minutes to confer, to re-light the welding torch, or make some further refinement in the equipment. In the masterful understatement of the Nautilus sailor, Bearden said later, "We ran into many problems of technique. We talked it over as we went along, developing the procedure bit by bit."

Altogether, Bearden and Kurrus were on the bridge in that gale for just about twelve hours—only two hours of that time actually spent in welding. To the amazement of every man in the crew, they successfully closed the gap. When they staggered down from the bridge, I met them in the Attack Centre. They were two of the coldest-looking men I have ever seen. Dr. Dobbins was on hand to supply them with medicinal alcohol.

The scope was straight, and the crack had been welded, but we were still not out of the wood. After the dry nitrogen had escaped from the barrel, the scope had filled with moist air. We all knew that immediately upon submerging, the scope would fog and be useless. Some means would have to be found to suck the moist air out of the barrel and create a vacuum, into which we could force more dry nitrogen. But how could we create a vacuum inside the periscope?

Another Nautilus sailor, Jimmy Youngblood, came up with the solution. In order to make Nautilus' steam plant operate efficiently, it is necessary that the steam itself exhaust into the main condensers, an area kept in a near-vacuum state. Youngblood suggested that a hose be run from the steam-condenser vacuum pumps, up through the ship to the periscope, and in that way a strong suction could be applied to the periscope barrel.

In a very short time the hose was rigged and the suction applied. Almost instantly the periscope was empty of air. A charge of dry nitrogen gas was shot through the periscope fitting, and then the whole process was repeated, just to make doubly sure we had cleaned the barrel of all moisture. The nitrogen fitting was sealed off, and after fifteen hours of work, number one periscope was almost as good as new.

It was the most amazing repair job at sea I had ever witnessed.

NINE

Compass Trouble

As soon as I could, I relayed the good news to Les Kelly on Trigger, informing him that we would continue operations as scheduled. Nautilus would dive at 0800 the following day and proceed under the ice to 83 degrees north and "further". We would be gone, I told him, between two and five days.

Kelly responded: "How far north does this imply you may go?"

I had not told a soul on the ship, but after our first excursion under the ice, and after the periscope had been repaired, I had worked up a set of figures—speed, distance, time, course—that would take us to the North Pole. It was 660 miles away and I figured that if all went well, we could make it there and back in four or five days. If it seemed at all feasible, I intended to go all the way.

However, I didn't want to tell Les Kelly this officially, so I replied jokingly: "Do not know how far north we will go. But we might get close enough to talk to Saint Nick."

We submerged and dived deep under the ice, travelling at a considerably greater speed than on our first expedition, completely unconcerned about the forbidding ceiling overhead. Most of our normal machinery, such as the reactor, the CO_2 scrubbers, and pumps, was functioning well. Dr. Lyon's special sonars were clicking away at a fast pace, accumulating an enormous storehouse of data that would keep polar experts busy for months. The temperature was a comfortable 72 degrees on board the Nautilus and the humidity hovered at about 50 per cent. Even my stateroom, which is ordinarily one of the coldest spots on the ship, was warm. The electricians had installed a special heater for this trip.

Once again life on board returned to normal, with the usual practical jokes and high jinks by the off-duty watch. This time a joke was conceived by the Chief Petty Officers, and the butt was a man named John Ropek, from the Navy Hydrographic Office. It is a good example of how, when there is no correlation with the outside environment, as on a nuclear submarine, people can get pretty confused about what time of day or night it is.

Ropek was, by profession, an ice forecaster. The Chiefs, with whom he bunked, had nicknamed him "Frosty, the Fearless Forecaster". One morning about ten o'clock, Ropek was lounging around in the Chiefs' Quarters, passing the time of day. The Chiefs, having plotted the prank in advance, got up one by one and began to yawn, saying they thought they'd turn in because it was getting pretty late in the evening. Soon they had all climbed into their bunks. Ropek, not at all sleepy then, followed suit. When Ropek was sound asleep, the Chiefs got up and went about their normal duties.

Ropek slept soundly all during the day. Late that afternoon he awoke, dressed, and came up to the Wardroom, where we were all just getting set to have our evening meal. It happened that we were having beef stew that night. When Ropek received his helping, he turned, puzzled, to Paul Early and asked:

"Do you always have stew for breakfast on Nautilus?"

That same evening, word reached the Wardroom that our hospital corpsman, or Major Keating, was writing notes, sealing them inside bottles, and firing them overboard through the garbage ejector. The notes, written in Russian, said: "Help, I am a prisoner in an American atomic submarine."

We sped on northward and in due time reached latitude 83 degrees north. A check of the compasses showed the magnetic one to be behaving erratically, our old-style gyro, designed for a maximum of 70 degrees north, wavering abnormally, and our new Mark 19 functioning quite well. Since there seemed to be no risk whatsoever involved, I ordered the Conning Officer to continue steering in a northerly direction toward the Pole. We passed 84, then 85 degrees north, with no significant change in compass performance. Soon the North Pole seemed within our grasp.

A couple of hours later, just before we had reached the 86th parallel, I was informed in urgent tones that both gyrocompasses had gone haywire. It happened so suddenly and so decisively that for a moment we stared in disbelief. Then quickly we realized that not the high latitude but something else had caused the abnormal gyrations. In a few seconds we discovered the cause of the trouble—the power supply to the compass had failed. A fuse had blown.

It couldn't be, I thought to myself. *Not after all this. A damned fuse. Is someone telling us to turn back?*

When a gyrocompass is shut off in normal latitudes, and then turned back on, about four hours are required for it to establish its equilibrium and "settle down". Since no-one had ever tried to re-start a gyrocompass at our extreme north latitude, we did not know how long it would take to find its head, or if, in fact, it would at all. We restored the power supply and began a period of watchful waiting. Meanwhile, we plotted our course as best we could by the magnetic compass, which was slowly swinging back and forth through an arc of about 60 degrees.

It was not a situation to cause panic, but it was a tense one. As Lieutenant Ken Carr put it at the time, "This reminds me of a guy who goes in to explore a cave, pulling a string with him from a reel at the entrance, so that he can find his way out. He gets almost where he wants to go and discovers that the string in his hand is broken."

Thinking that a sharp turn might disturb the re-started gyrocompass even more, we continued on a northerly course. Where before we had been cautious with our navigation, now we were exacting. A simple mistake at that latitude, where longitudinal lines begin to converge, could throw us into the dreaded game of longitude roulette. Conceivably, we could be led into the wrong ocean or even, worse, up against an ice-locked coastline. The ship's navigators were subjected to a barrage of friendly jokes about liberty in Alaska and, inevitably, Murmansk.

Shortly after we passed latitude 87 degrees north, about 180 miles from the North Pole—an estimate we were able to check later—I gave the order to execute a sweeping, gradual turn. I regretted that we had not reached the Pole, but considered that to go any further would expose the ship and the crew to undue risks.

After we had completed the turn, a friendly argument broke out among the crew over who had been closest to the Pole. Lieutenant Frank Wadsworth, who had deliberately gone as far forward in the forward Torpedo Room as he could, promptly claimed the honour. But after a swift and detailed calculation, the men in the stern demonstrated that in a turn, the stern of the ship actually sweeps farther out—in this case north—than the bow. The men in the stern were about to walk off with the prize when a man who had been sitting on the port side piped up. He contended that in a turn to starboard he would have been closer to the Pole than anyone else on the ship. After due consideration of this complex and highly controversial question, I had to rule in favour of the man who had been sitting on the port side.

Few navigators and quartermasters have worked harder or under more trying circumstances than Lieutenant Bill Lalor and his men on the Nautilus who plotted our course south to the edge of the ice. The Mark 19 did not "settle down" for almost seven hours. During that period we steered by the swinging magnetic compass, hoping all the while that it was not actually "walking," and taking us in large circles around the Pole.

Even after it settled, we could not be certain that the master compass was accurately aligned. We navigated by scraps of information, by "averaging out" the swing of the magnetic compass and by guesswork. There was little sleep for those who were engaged in this task. Fortunately, all other machinery continued to perform with exceptional efficiency—we discovered, for example, that in colder water our reactor produced more speed—and my mind was left free to concentrate on one problem of navigation.

Much to my dismay we soon found that we had in fact been a victim of longitude roulette. Just as we expected to find the gradually shoaling ocean plain that leads into the open waters of the Greenland Sea, we suddenly ran into very shallow water. We had noted that the ice was much more compact than we expected, and that the water temperature was much colder. A quick analysis of our environment showed what was later confirmed—we had run almost into the ice-locked coast of northern Greenland. I ordered a 90-degree course change to the left. After what appeared to be ages we were in deep water again.

A day later we cleared the outer edge of the ice pack. We had been submerged under the ice for a period of seventy-four hours and had covered a distance of almost a thousand miles. Dr. Lyon's instruments had obtained readings totalling tens of thousands, and in the case of precise bottom soundings, millions. We had not come as close to the Pole as we hoped. However, we believed that, ultimately, the navigational knowledge we gained in high latitudes would be of far greater value to other nuclear submarines that might venture under the ice than the mere fact of reaching the Pole. As far as records go, we did establish one. We travelled farther north than the ice-locked drifters Fram and Sedov and, of course, much farther north than any other ship under its own power.

We made contact with Trigger, and after a day of resting and relaxing while she steamed sixty miles under the ice—a considerable achievement for a conventional submarine—we got under way for a third and final foray beneath the pack. Having discharged our primary mission of making a deep penetration, this time we played around, steaming as we chose in squares and circles, zipping back and forth with abandon, while Dr. Lyon gathered a continuous record of data.

When the day was half over, we spied a good-sized polynia, and since the gale had blown itself out during our deep penetration, we decided to surface. Once again we manoeuvred

Nautilus carefully beneath the ice and then inched our way up. Soon the periscope broke water, and I found myself inspecting a scene few men had seen from the ground level. Broken, jumbled, desolate ice stretched to the horizon in every direction.

The polynia was just large enough to hold us. The water was calm, and though the ice was in motion around us, we were not concerned. If it closed in we would simply "pull the cork" and descend beneath it. The ice itself was not strong enough to crush the hull of our submarine. While Dr. Lyon and his assistant were busy taking sea-bottom samples, I put John Krawczyk, who is Nautilus' official photographer, over the side in a rubber life raft to take pictures. Half the crew volunteered to row. I was thinking during this time, had we been so equipped and so ordered, we could have fired any number of guided missiles.

Nautilus, in effect, had opened up a new and fascinating chapter of naval warfare. Our cruise, from a military standpoint, had demonstrated that nuclear ships could operate in this wilderness in relative safety and comfort and, until the Soviet Union developed its own nuclear submarines, completely unopposed by hostile naval forces.

Already the Navy had in various stages of development four revolutionary nuclear-powered, missile-launching submarines, which Admiral Rickover described as versatile "underwater satellites," capable of unleashing a devastating attack against the Russians, should they launch a war against us. Such a force, Rickover said, could operate in the Arctic Ocean and even beneath the ice. A glance at a polar-projection map will show that this vast, unfriendly area would be an ideal base for the underwater satellite with its arsenal of long-range missiles.

Most of the Soviet heartland could be reached with only 1,500-mile missiles—fired from open stretches in the ice such as ours. Rickover had said, "Because it is able to hide and even lie still against sonar, the atomic missile submarine cannot be easily traced by the enemy. Search radar would be helpless against it. The enemy would be in the position of trying to find a black cat on a vast and empty plain on a moonless and starless night." It was already clear to me that in the white, trackless Arctic, an area denied to surface vessels, it would be even more difficult to detect a missile-firing atomic submarine, and harder to kill it if detected, since the submarine could use the thick ice floes as a bomb shelter. Clearly, our cruise had proved that this eerie but important new deterrent concept was militarily feasible.

After two hours of activity in our remote, private lake in the ice, we submerged, and in two days, having logged over two hundred miles, we returned to the edge of the pack and again made contact with Trigger. Then we set a submerged course for England.

It was the prophetic imagination of Jules Verne that first popularized the concept of submarine activity under the polar ice, with his mythical submarine Nautilus. Once again, the real-life Nautilus, the creation of another man of great imagination and foresight, Admiral Rickover, had made one of Verne's dreams a reality. As the Nautilus headed toward warmer waters, we, her crew, felt a sense of achievement at having greatly expanded man's scientific knowledge of the Arctic area. However, we had little time to reflect on it, for almost immediately we began to prepare for "combat" in the STRIKEBACK manoeuvre which lay just ahead.

By coincidence, en route to England, Nautilus fulfilled another Jules Verne dream. Just south of the Arctic Circle, Nautilus clocked her 60,000th submerged mile. Using the popularly accepted measure of three miles to the league, it meant that the ship, with only one refuelling, had steamed "20,000 Leagues Under the Sea".

TEN

A Conference at the White House

In STRIKEBACK, and in a later special exercise with the cream of the British anti-submarine forces, Nautilus performed well, and many ships were theoretically sent to the bottom. The British Navy was tremendously impressed with the capabilities of Nautilus. So much so, that future British sea power may be built around a core of nuclear-powered submarines. The British already have one nuclear-powered submarine, the Dreadnought, under construction. The complete power plant will be furnished by the United States under terms of a bilateral atomic agreement between the United States and Britain.

In late October we turned west, and by the end of the month Nautilus was home again, in New London.

Not many days after our arrival I flew to Washington to brief the staff of the Chief of Naval Operations on STRIKEBACK and our polar operation. I had already filed an official scientific report on the ice probe, recommending further operations in the area. It was my feeling that with advanced navigational equipment and improved compasses, a nuclear-powered submarine could easily reach the North Pole, although I did not recommend the Pole as a specific objective.

It was almost dark by the time I left the Pentagon. I was a little discouraged because I felt I had failed that afternoon to impress the audience with the significance of what Nautilus had just done. As I walked wearily down the steps of the Mall entrance, I saw Captain Peter Aurand, the President's Naval Aide, whom I had met casually six months before. We shook hands, and he asked if he could give me a lift into town. As

An inspection party took out a dinghy when Nautilus surfaced in a gap in
the ice pack during the 1957 cruise.

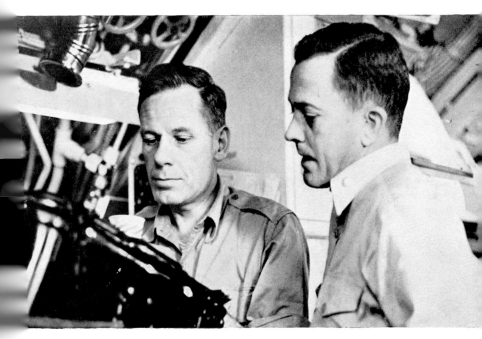

Dr. Waldo Lyon (left) and Commander Anderson watch reports on the
ice detection equipment.

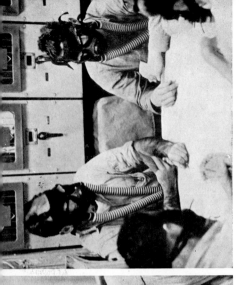

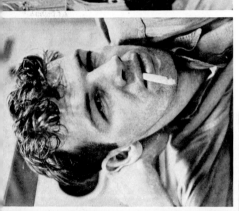

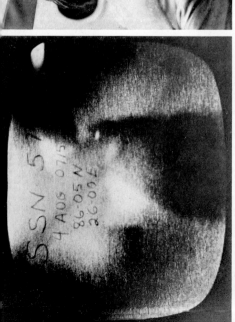

(*above left*) The ship's closed-circuit television screen reveals a water hole and an ice floe overhead.

(*above centre*) Richard Bearden, one of the two welders who worked in a gale for 12 hours to repair the damaged periscope during the 1957 cruise.

(*above right*) Members of the crew wearing emergency breathing apparatus as a precaution against fire during the under-ice probe.

(*left*) Enlisted men off duty relaxing in the crew's mess.

we crossed the Potomac, headed toward the White House, he asked what Nautilus had been up to lately, so I told him briefly of our probe under the ice pack, and of the fact that we had come within 180 miles of the North Pole.

Aurand was very interested in the details of this trip and asked whether I would, without telling anyone, come to his White House office on the following day. I replied, of course, that I would.

The next day I gave Aurand a complete briefing on the trip. He grasped at once the tremendous potential of nuclear submarine operations in the Arctic. Moreover, it was a time when solid proof of United States technical and scientific development was badly needed: sputniks were whirling overhead, and the Russians were reaping a rich propaganda harvest. This fact may have led to Aurand's next question:

"Do you think you could take the Nautilus completely around the world submerged?"

"It is just a question of devoting time and nuclear fuel to it," I replied.

Very soon our eyes turned to a huge chart of the world on the wall of Captain Aurand's office. The avid discussion that followed kept me on the edge of my chair. We talked of Nautilus circumnavigating the globe by various undersea routes and then, inevitably, about a trip from ocean to ocean across the Pole itself, beneath the ice pack. The more we pondered this latter possibility, the more intrigued we became.

To be frank, at the beginning of our discussion of a possible trip across the top of the world, I was thinking of something in the future—say two or three years hence. I had suggested in my official report of the 1957 cruise that submerged Arctic exploration be carried out with "measured acceleration," that is, on a step-by-step basis. Considering the inherent dangers and the unenthusiastic reaction in some circles to our 1957 voyage, it did not occur to me that official backing for an immediate trip from the Pacific to the Atlantic could be obtained. But I had not reckoned with the imagination and enthusiasm of

F

the White House itself, nor with the drive of Admiral Burke and his staff.

Aurand cautioned me that secrecy was paramount. Then he asked if I could return in about a week to brief the full White House staff on our 1957 cruise.

"Anything you say, sir," I replied.

Then I was off to New London to rejoin the ship. I said nothing about my visit to the White House. A week later, I was back in Washington. About thirty members of the White House staff, including Sherman Adams and James Hagerty, attended the briefing.

James Hagerty posed the question which Aurand had asked me earlier, one that I am sure was on the minds of many people:

"Can you take that ship of yours around the world submerged?"

"Yes, sir," I replied again. "It is mainly a matter of allowing the necessary time and nuclear fuel."

Mr. Hagerty nodded his head and walked away, obviously deep in thought. A dozen feet away, he wheeled around and came back, grinning broadly, and with a twinkle in his eye said, "Thanks—thanks a lot."

Although nothing had been said officially or unofficially, I came away from that meeting convinced that the White House had more than a casual interest in the Nautilus and her polar cruise. I followed Captain Aurand back to his office and there, for about an hour, we again discussed possible future polar operations. We agreed that the most significant aspect of any round-the-world cruise would be a journey from the Pacific to the Atlantic by the under-ice route across the North Pole, thus attaining the goal of centuries of explorations, a north-west passage.

When I left the White House, Captain Aurand again cautioned me not to reveal that I had been there, nor to discuss with anyone a possible transpolar trip for the Nautilus. Back in New London, against the possibility that the White House would generate some kind of transpolar proposal, I put in a formal letter to the Pentagon, suggesting that Nautilus make a second polar probe in 1958. If the White House discussions resulted in a firm plan, we would need additional navigating and sonar equipment. Approval for a routine polar probe in 1958 for Nautilus would give us an excuse to begin installing it.

As I contemplated this Top Secret voyage, I went through a period of painstaking self-examination. It seemed incredible that people had actually been talking in terms of it. I reflected on the 1957 cruise, on what we had learned and what we had yet to learn. On the basis of that trip, if it had been left up to me, I would not have recommended a transpolar crossing in 1958. Yet I had told the White House I thought it could be done.

I then contemplated the thousand and one things we ought to be doing to get ready but, sworn to secrecy as I was, I could do nothing but study and wait. Six weeks passed, with no official word. All I knew—and that from a brief and necessarily sketchy phone call from Aurand—was that "things were generating".

Meanwhile, in the wake of my visit to the Pentagon, top naval officers had begun to think in terms of Hagerty's question. A small group of officers was ordered to make a feasibility study. Their conclusion was, like mine, yes. Shortly thereafter, Chief of Naval Operations Admiral Burke proposed to the President that Nautilus attempt the trip the following summer.

The President's reaction can only be described as completely enthusiastic. Our proposed polar transit became a sort of pet project of the President's. I feel, personally, that it was due largely to his unflagging interest that the trip was successfully completed.

The voyage, then, became the most Top Secret peace-time naval operation in history. The reasons for complete secrecy were twofold. First, Nautilus, by going through the Bering Strait, would pass well clear of Soviet territorial limits, but possibly near her submarine operating areas, and there was a risk— admittedly remote—that some incident might occur. Secondly all hands felt that it was wiser to make the journey, if possible, first, and announce it after it had been completed, thus avoiding another Vanguard fiasco. As it turned out, only a handful of people in the entire government were acquainted with the details.

In January I received a mysterious, urgent telephone call from the Pentagon, concerning, I was told, a matter that was "too sensitive to talk about over the telephone". I was ordered to report as soon as possible to the office of Rear Admiral L. R. Daspit, Director of Undersea Warfare. When I rushed aboard the overnight train for Washington I was genuinely apprehensive. I thought, "What have I done wrong now?"

At the Pentagon I joined Captain Frank Walker, head of the Submarine Warfare Branch, and Commander M. G. ("Duke") Bayne. We hurried to Admiral Daspit's office. The Admiral asked his Chief Yeoman to leave the office, and then he shut the door. After we sat down, he looked at me and asked: "Anderson, what do you think about taking the Nautilus from one ocean to another across the North Pole?" Then he told me of Admiral Burke's proposal to the President and the latter's keen interest.

By then I had given more than considerable thought and study to the idea from a strictly operational standpoint. There was no doubt in my mind that Nautilus could penetrate the ice safely and efficiently from the Greenland-Spitsbergen side of the pack, as we had done in 1957. The water there was quite deep. I knew that the really formidable problem lay on the other side, in the Bering Strait and the Chukchi Sea, a small body of water lying between the Strait and the Arctic Ocean.

Viewed from the top of the world, this area resembles a huge funnel, with the spout—the Bering Strait—lying to the south. There the ice is far more irregular and hazardous than that on the Greenland side. Blown southward against the walls of the funnel, represented by Alaska and Siberia, the ice "chokes up" at the narrow mouth. In fact, it jams, layer upon layer against these rugged coastlines, and as a result is far

thicker than the ice near the North Pole. To make matters
worse, the waters of the Strait and Chukchi Sea are quite
shallow, averaging not more than 120 feet, much too shallow
for ordinary submarine operations. If a submarine in those
waters encountered deep-hanging ice, it might not be able to
get beneath or around it. It would be a hair-raising problem
of threading through dangerous ice, seeking out the few deeper
ocean-floor valleys which lead northward into the Arctic
Basin.

From a purely operational standpoint, the question was:
could a submarine negotiate this track in the face of possible
poor weather and navigational errors? In my mind, as I sat
there before Admiral Daspit, I could envisage Nautilus creeping
through that unknown area, fathometers sounding the distance
to the bottom and to the ice overhead. There would not be
many feet to spare in either direction. It would be something
like a small boy trying to squirm under a low-hanging fence,
with the big difference that there is nothing small about
Nautilus—long as a city block and four thousand tons submerged.

Yet it could be done. I was certain of that. And I said
so.

One conference followed upon the other. Dr. Waldo Lyon
was summoned to Washington. He concurred in my decision
that the trip should be made from Pacific to Atlantic, tackling,
in effect, the toughest end of the transit first. Neither then nor
later could we be absolutely certain that we could get through.
Our first effort would be in the nature of a tentative probe.
If we could get through—and I was determined to do so if at
all possible—we would go all the way. If we found the ice too
dangerous, we would re-evaluate our plans on the spot. My
orders, I knew, would tell me not to subject Nautilus and the
crew to undue hazards.

The remaining question was when to make this first trip, in
winter or summer? During winter, the polar ice pack extends
well down into the narrow, shallow Bering Strait. In the
warmer months it recedes almost to the edge of the deep Arctic

Basin. Future operations may prove that my judgement was wrong, but based on the little knowledge of the ice that we had then, it seemed logical to launch the trip in the summer, thus reducing to a minimum our cruising time under ice in very shallow water.

The date was tentatively set for June 8.

ELEVEN

Double Talk and Frenzied Preparations

When I returned to New London, I summoned my new Executive Officer, Lieutenant Commander Frank Adams, my Chief Engineer, Lieutenant Paul Early, and my new Navigator, Lieutenant Shep Jenks, to my stateroom, and after warning them that the conversation was to be considered Top Secret, I told them of the momentous events which had been taking place in Washington. The four of us then tackled what is undoubtedly the toughest job I have experienced in my naval service: preparing Nautilus for a transpolar voyage in utter secrecy.

To justify the installation of our new sonar and navigating equipment, which could not possibly be concealed, Admiral Burke approved a "cover operation plan". The Navy announced that in the summer of 1958 the nuclear-powered submarines Nautilus and Skate, and the conventional submarine Halfbeak, were to engage in "Arctic Operations". No other details were revealed. The impression was left that Nautilus would, as she had the previous summer, make a polar probe in the Greenland-Spitsbergen area.

Next, to justify our trip to the Pacific, where we would stage for our transpolar voyage, Admiral Burke passed along the word that the Nautilus would make a spring voyage to the West Coast to familiarize anti-submarine warfare units with the capabilities of a nuclear-powered submarine. Ports of call would be Balboa, Panama, San Diego, San Francisco, and Seattle. On June 7, he said, Nautilus would begin her return trip to the East Coast, departing from Seattle and making a twenty-six-day submerged cruise back to Panama. On a long submerged run of that kind, independent of the earth's atmosphere, we could turn down, without causing suspicion, the usual requests from scientists and naval personnel for a ride, on the grounds that our oxygen supply was limited.

Under this plan Admiral Burke could also furnish a plausible excuse to the many anti-submarine units that usually exercise with us when we come into their jurisdiction. It would be a long trip, the Chief of Naval Operations could say, on a route that would take Nautilus many miles from all Pacific bases. We would be busy making atmospheric tests and studying the problems of very long-range submerged cruises, the results of which would be important to the Polaris submarine programme. In this particular case, Admiral Burke could say, it would be better not to burden Nautilus with too many jobs.

Under the "cover operation" plan, Nautilus would theoretically return to New London in July, make final preparations, and depart, with Skate and Halfbeak, for the Greenland area in late July or early August.

In retrospect, our efforts to carry out the cover operation plan seem almost as trying as the trip itself. The only officer in New London to whom I could talk freely was Rear Admiral F. B. Warder, Commander of all Atlantic submarines. Since I do not like to mislead my crew deliberately, I was careful to make myself scarce just prior to any occasion when the subject of our future operations might arise.

The first piece of special equipment to arrive was a complex device called an inertial navigator, which is as sensitive and intricate as an electronic brain. It was designed by North American Aviation engineers to guide their Navaho missile from continent to continent. It stored up information on speed, course, and other factors, and would furnish us with a continuous reading on our position.

The inertial navigator was installed aboard Nautilus by mid-April. North American engineers, working in secrecy and under a severe time limit, did, I think, a magnificent job. When I first saw this amazing array of electronics (the connecting circuits are "printed" in gold), I had only one reaction:

"It will never work." I was decisively proved wrong. After the bugs had been worked out, the inertial navigator, or N6A, as it was called, kept us precisely informed of our position at all times. This device, when it becomes available in large quantities for commercial shipping, will revolutionize the ancient art of sea navigation. It will also be a valuable piece of equipment for our Polaris submarines. In order to place a ballistic missile on target, it is imperative to know the exact launching position.

While this work was in progress, the engineers of Sperry Gyroscope installed an additional compass on the Nautilus and especially modified the other two for high-latitude operations. Fred Braddon, their Chief Engineer, spent hours discussing with Jenks and me how to overcome the problems of polar navigation. At the same time, Dr. Lyon's men arrived with six new sonar instruments. One of these was built exclusively for the Nautilus. It was vastly more sensitive and efficient than those we had used on our 1957 cruise and would enable us to make the first truly detailed scientific analysis of sea ice. Electric Boat workmen swarmed about Nautilus twenty-four hours a day.

Both the Electric Boat employees and the crew of the Nautilus, we sensed, were curious about the frenzied activity. If Nautilus was not going on an Arctic cruise until late July or August, and we would stop in New London before the trip, then why all the rush preparations now? Why not install the new gear later? Our excuse was that there would be very little time for gear installation during the mythical stop-over. It would be better to complete all modifications now, so that we could make final preparations for the "Greenland" ice cruise in a relaxed mood.

When Rear Admiral Warder and I saw that even this story had not removed all doubts, we deliberately arranged a conference with Electric Boat workmen, to discuss some work items that would be accomplished in the late July "stop-over". Following the conference, Captain A. C. Smith, the supervisor of shipbuilding at Groton, published for all Electric Boat employees a fictional schedule, showing Nautilus' arrival date in Panama on the return trip home. Arrangements were made for Electric Boat supervisors to fly to Panama to join the ship for the trip back to New London, so the phony work items would be expedited.

In late February, Rear Admiral Warder ordered a conference on the polar operations of Nautilus, Skate, and Halfbeak. By then practically every Arctic expert had been intrigued by the possibility of submarine operations in the polar area, and they came in droves to the conference. I briefed my officers, all of whom had been advised of our true intentions by this time. We prepared a fictional operational schedule for Nautilus to enter the ice from Greenland, and sat through the conference, being fussy and particular about this point or that, thoroughly concealing our real plans.

To be entirely fair, a voyage of this sort should be made strictly by volunteers. In preparing for our departure from the East Coast, I believe I discharged my obligation in that respect. After the routine announcement that Nautilus, Skate, and Halfbeak would participate in Arctic operations, I requested my junior officers to try out their men quietly with this question: "Are there any who prefer to take leave or to stay on the submarine tender during the ice operations?" Not one Nautilus sailor accepted the offer.

I felt a slight sense of guilt because the Nautilus crew had always been a close-mouthed group and I trust them implicitly down to the last man. But there is always that inadvertent slip which can happen to anyone, regardless of rank or rating. The fact is, the way to keep something Top Secret is to tell as few people as possible. I rationalized, too, telling myself that it would be a crushing disappointment to the crew if, by some chance, our trip were cancelled after they had been told the polar transit was a probability.

Towards the end, in spite of our careful planning, many of the Nautilus crewmen, I believe, were downright suspicious. For example, at the last minute, when we loaded on board cold-weather clothing and anti-freeze for the fresh-water system of the auxiliary Diesel engine, one of the Chiefs asked, "Now if we're just going on a spring trip to California, then why do we need these items? They are certainly things that can easily be loaded at the last minute."

Again we repeated our stock answer: "Let's do as many things as we can now." But, feeling that something further was needed to convince the crew, we put in motion another counter-rumour plan.

One morning Adams called the crew to quarters and announced that I had obtained permission, on our trip from the West Coast back to Panama, to dip down and cross the equator. He suggested that since it would be the first time a nuclear submarine had crossed the equator, the crew ought to plan a super-colossal celebration to initiate the Pollywogs as Shellbacks. Those in charge of this celebration which, of course, would never take place, went so far as to have special certificates printed for the ceremony. After this announcement, we were certain, no man in the crew expected to enter the ice from the Pacific.

One problem which now seems minor but at the time presented a major challenge was that of obtaining charts and publications on the area from Alaska to Portland, England. We knew that if we put in a routine request for these, it would arouse suspicion in the Hydrographic Office. Duke Bayne in CNO's office handled that one. He simply requested, in CNO's name, charts of the entire Arctic area, making it appear that CNO was interested in a general study of the top of the globe. Shep Jenks flew down to Washington to pick up the material. He kept it locked in a safe, and whenever he wanted to study, he would slip into my stateroom and bolt the door.

We discovered that, other than aircraft navigation charts which we had used the year before and a published Russian chart showing some soundings, which later proved to be completely inaccurate, there were still no charts available of the Arctic Basin area. At our request, CNO asked the Hydrographic Office to prepare a special set. CNO was told they couldn't possibly be made ready before late July. CNO replied that he needed them "for study" in May, and to see that they were done on a "crash" basis. These charts, many of which contained soundings we had made on our 1957 cruise, were ultimately delivered to Nautilus by Top Secret Mail in San Francisco, just before we left for the final staging point, Seattle.

From a personal standpoint, the extreme security measures caused me many anxious and painful moments. I believe I alienated many of my professional friends because of the necessity of clamming up suddenly, or talking in circles about our future operations.

At home it was pretty much the same. My tempo had stepped up drastically. Every few days, it seemed, I was racing off to Washington on some trumped-up excuse or another. The telephone rang in the middle of the night. I—and all of us who knew—talked in guarded language that must have sounded like some fantastic new brand of slang. At home I spent a great deal of my time in the library, closeted with charts and books.

The year before, some of the wives had been told, or had guessed, that Nautilus would make a trip under the ice pack. Since the Navy had announced plans to operate Nautilus, Skate, and Halfbeak in the Arctic in the summer of 1958, of course, the wives knew we were headed back for the ice pack. However, as time went on, I could sense that Bonny knew that our operation entailed more than we had done the year before, more even than going to the North Pole, and I could tell that she surmised the trip probably would come well within her definition of "dangerous". However, Bonny knows well the merit of silence on delicate matters. Aware that I was closely guarding the operation, she did not ask me point-blank where we were headed. I was glad of that.

Almost before we realized it, our day of departure from New London arrived. Just after dark on the twenty-fifth of April, we backed out of our slip at Electric Boat, and headed down the Thames River to Long Island Sound. When we reached deep water, we submerged and set a course for Panama.

TWELVE

Ill Omens

A good baseball manager can
usually sense, and often predict fairly accurately, whether or
not his team will have a good day on the diamond. Similarly,
a ship's captain, through certain small observations or, perhaps,
intuition, can tell if his ship will have a good cruise. I am no
more superstitious than the ordinary seafarer, but certain
signs, such as a fair wind, I believe, can make a difference. I
remember how it was when I was skipper of Wahoo, operating
from Pearl Harbour, for example. When I saw porpoises
playing around the bow as we left port, I had a good feeling,
a feeling that our cruise would be a success. When I saw no
porpoises, I felt just the opposite. And my predictions were
usually fairly accurate.

Under way for Panama, I began instinctively to look for
the signs. Then, and for many weeks to follow, they appeared
to be negative. We seemed to be plagued with a series of
problems, mostly mechanical, that clearly demonstrated
that Nautilus was not up to peak.

En route to Panama, with the reactor working perfectly, we
discovered that a tiny salt-water leak had developed in one of
the steam condensers. A leak of this kind—we estimated it
was no larger than a human hair—is not unusual on a submarine. This one, however, was emptying into a critical piece
of machinery that was not specifically designed to resist the
corrosive effects of salt water. If it continued, we knew, there
was a danger that it could ultimately cause a major breakdown
of the propulsion machinery. If this occurred under the ice, it
could be a catastrophe.

93

Our Engineering Officer, Paul Early, and his team of experts combed through the pipes and valves with the thoroughness of Sherlock Holmes. According to Early's calculation of the number of tubes and fittings, the leak might be occurring at any one of about ten thousand places, many of them impossible to reach without literally tearing the ship apart. They checked as many as they could, but they could not find the leak. Slowly, to my great concern, the chloride level in the condensers began to climb.

At the same time we noted that the air in the ship was not as pure as we like to maintain it. There were inexplicable "fumes" circulating throughout the ship, with a high concentration in the Engine Room and Manoeuvring Room. At first we thought it might be paint fumes, since a good deal of the below-deck machinery and spaces had been freshly painted during our preparations in New London. But these fumes did not diminish, as one might expect of ordinary paint odours. On the contrary, as we approached Panama, they increased. By the time we reached Balboa, the eyes of the men who stood watch in the Engine Room and Manoeuvring Room were watery and red. McNally satirized this situation with a cartoon showing a Nautilus sailor debarking in Panama with dark glasses on, tears running down his cheeks, probing along a sidewalk with a cane. A couple of elderly women standing aside were saying, "It's the saddest sight I ever saw."

But for me it was no humorous matter. Something was wrong. Seriously wrong.

Our stop in Panama was brief—about two days. One evening I had an opportunity to renew an old friendship with Captain Rollo Miller, a submariner, who invited my Exec and me to dinner. Miller asked Adams and me if we would dine with him on our "return" to Panama in July. Since we could not divulge our real plans, there was nothing to do but accept. Nautilus crewmen, then a little shy of money, put down payments on gifts which they intended to pick up on the "return" trip. John Krawczyk was tickled pink with a new camera lens he saw in a shop. He made a small partial payment and later wrote that he would be back in July to pay in full and collect the lens.

We left Panama on May 4. After a brief run on the surface we reached deep water and submerged. Almost instantly the engineers noted that the fumes had increased considerably. In a very few minutes their eyes began to water again.

At about 1500 Lieutenant Bill Lalor, Main Propulsion Officer, climbed down into the machinery spaces to inspect a small sea-water leak in one of the propeller shafts. Coming forward again, he noted, not without considerable concern, smoke drifting up from the area near the port main turbine. "It was about as much as you'd expect to see from a man smoking a cigar," he recalled later. But there was no man below smoking a cigar. Lalor relayed word to Lieutenant Steven White and Chief Stuart Nelson, who were standing watch in the Manoeuvring Room, where the controls for the reactor and the steam system are located.

At first it was believed that oil was probably dripping through a connection on to one of the "hot lines" in the steam system, a relatively simple matter. Nelson passed the word to one of the enlisted engineers to go below, wipe up the oil, and tighten the leaking connection.

But about that time it became apparent that this was no simple oil leak. Smoke began billowing into the upper level of the Engine Room in great quantity, blinding the men on watch. A few minutes later Lieutenant White called the Control Room and reported: "We've got a lot of smoke back here. People are having trouble seeing." Word was then officially passed: "Fire in the Engine Room." I headed aft.

Lalor and Paul Early, followed by sailors who had been watching the afternoon movie—Pilcher, Aquizap, Boswell, Holland, Kurrus, Bearden, McNally, and others—also rushed to the Engine Room. As Lalor recalled later, "What I saw was hard to believe. In only a few minutes since my departure, the whole space was clouded with acrid smoke. The men on watch were crying uncontrollably, coughing, and very much concerned."

Nautilus was now fully alerted. Every man on board was standing by to render assistance. By the time I reached the Engine Room, the smoke made it difficult to see or breathe. Most of the men in the compartment had draped dampened towels over their faces. Others had donned goggles and other eye-protecting devices.

The first task was to find the source of the smoke. Holland and McNally, wearing two of the four special smoke masks we had on board, scampered down the ladder to the machinery spaces below, feeling their way through the smoke, carefully avoiding the boiling hot lines of steam propulsion machinery. Other men followed, lugging CO_2 fire extinguishers. I ordered the port shaft stopped and its steam turbine cooled down. We had come up to snorkel depth and were trying to suck the smoke out with the snorkel, but with little success.

It was now clear to me that a serious situation had developed and that it was necessary to take Nautilus to the surface. Once there, we could open the Engine Room hatch and through it part of the smoke would escape. In addition, we could light off our small emergency Diesel engine, which takes its air supply directly from the Engine Room spaces. That would suck off more of the smoke.

I gave the order to surface and to open the Engine Room hatch. Fortunately the seas were calm and no water splashed down. In fact, it was so calm that I permitted the men who had been overcome by smoke to go up on the deck for a breath of fresh air.

Meanwhile, Holland and McNally were crawling through the maze of pipes, valves, and turbines down below, seeking the source of the smoke. They reminded me of two men fighting a nest of rattlesnakes. At last they found the fire. The insulation, or lagging, as we call it, around the port high-pressure turbine, after several years of operation had, like a wick, gradually become oil-soaked. High-speed running in warm tropical waters, we reasoned, had finally caused it to catch fire.

Using jack-knives and pliers, Holland and McNally began tearing the smouldering insulation from the turbine housing.

When they ripped off the first chunk, flames three to four feet high leaped up, almost searing their faces. The men manning the fire extinguishers brought the liquid foam to bear, but with great care since, in such confined quarters, they could easily have squirted CO_2 on their companions. The foam instantly freezes anything it comes into contact with, and it could have seriously injured those trying to rip away the lagging.

Men were coughing and gagging by that time, and no man could remain inside the compartment for more than ten or fifteen minutes. One of the men, Pilcher, staggered topside and collapsed on the deck. He said later that he had no recollection of going topside and has no idea how he got there. Some men were nauseated. Fighting through the smoke and after considerable probing, two of the men found the controls for the auxiliary Diesel and lighted it off. This helped reduce the smoke. I ordered Larch and Callahan to stay on the deck topside and make sure no-one fell overboard.

Down below, where the flaming insulation was gradually being ripped off the turbine, man relieved man every few minutes or so. It was a miserable, dangerous, backbreaking, seemingly endless task. The bilges were soon chock-full of charred insulation and the white foam of the CO_2 extinguishers. Every man connected with the engine spaces and others, such as the electricians, took a turn. Gradually, after four hours, the last of the inflamed lagging was removed and doused. The fire was out.

That it did not become more serious was due to the work of many fine Nautilus crewmen. Two men who played leading roles in stamping out the fire—Kurrus and Bearden—were the same two who performed the remarkable periscope welding job on the 1957 cruise.

Our greatest potential danger beneath the ice pack—fire—had risen up to slap me in the face. That night, as I lay tossing in my bunk, I shuddered to think what might have happened to us if that small fire had occurred beneath the ice, in a place where we could not break our way to the surface. The answer was all too obvious: Nautilus would have been lost.

G

I realized then that we would have to devote more attention to fire hazards. A thorough inspection would have to be conducted. We would have to have some kind of special breathing apparatus to protect the crew in case fire of that kind broke out while we were submerged under the pack.

When we reached San Francisco I hastily conferred with representatives of the Bureau of Ships and in an amazingly short time they had installed on board Nautilus special, smoke-proof breathing apparatus that we could, through a system of regulators, connect to the air supply we carry on board to blow the ballast tanks dry. However, there was time enough to install only enough units for the watch—the men on duty actually controlling the ship. If we had a fire under the ice, the ship could probably be saved by these men, but the remaining two-thirds of the crew might perish. I ordered a fire-prevention programme the likes of which no submarine crew had ever seen before.

Meanwhile, during our stop-over in the Navy Yard, the insulation on the starboard turbine, which was also oil-soaked, was removed. Working around the clock, workmen fabricated new lagging for both turbines.

At the same time, legions of engineers, workmen, and high Navy gold braid came aboard to grapple with our most serious problem: the damnable, persistent salt-water leak in the condenser. The best men in the nation were trying to solve this riddle, and they were not making much headway. The ship was pulled into dock and gone over inch by inch. But no-one could find the leak. I was becoming increasingly concerned, not so much that the leak would cause us a major disaster beneath the ice, but that someone in Washington would consider the risk too great and, after all our preparations and hope, cancel the trip.

There were many weird—and sometimes absurd—events that arose because of the Top Secret nature of our voyage, but few to equal a personal experience I had at this time. In San Francisco we had received our Arctic Basin charts by Top Secret Mail, but I did not want to trust our Operation SUN-

SHINE orders to this means of communication. I knew that Dr. Lyon was in Washington on a last-minute trip, so I called the Pentagon and made arrangements for Dr. Lyon to bring the orders back to the West Coast with him. I would fly down to Los Angeles—on the pretext of visiting the North American plant to talk with engineers about the inertial navigator—meet Dr. Lyon at the International Airport during his change of planes for San Diego, and personally receive the orders from him.

My air reservations were delayed and by the time I arrived in Los Angeles that evening, wearing civilian clothes, Dr. Lyon had already gone on to San Diego with the orders. I reached him by telephone and asked if he could come out to the San Diego airport and bring the orders.

Then I walked over to the ticket counter and told the agent I wanted a round-trip ticket to San Diego. I got a reservation on a plane that flew down to San Diego, stayed on the ground fifteen minutes, then returned to Los Angeles.

"When will you be returning?" asked the ticket agent. "Perhaps I can arrange your return reservation now."

"I want to come back on that same airplane," I replied.

"It will only be there fifteen minutes," said the agent. By now he was eyeing me sharply. Only then did it occur to me that my journey to San Diego was somewhat out of the ordinary. *He probably thinks I'm going down there to pick up a batch of dope*, I thought.

No further questions were asked, however. I boarded the plane, flew to San Diego, and Dr. Lyon was there waiting for me at the airport. We sat briefly on an out-of-the-way bench. After I had signed for the orders, we squared away several pressing items. I was back aboard the plane when it took off to return to Los Angeles, and back aboard Nautilus just before sunrise.

The engineers at Mare Island were anxious to continue searching Nautilus for the pesky leak. But time was closing in. I knew that if I didn't leave then, we might spend a month tied to the dock. I had confidence in the ship. Even if the condenser failed completely, I was hopeful that we could still make it across the top. Abruptly I announced to the local naval commander—a man far superior in rank to me—that I was taking Nautilus out to sea the following morning.

Unfortunately I could not reveal to him just why it was necessary that we move on. When we left the Navy Yard, several of the men and naval officers who had worked so hard to find the leak were pretty peeved at one W. R. Anderson. Under way and still leaking, but better the masters of our own fate, we set a submerged course for our final staging point, Seattle. I continued to look for signs that would indicate a successful voyage. No porpoises had chosen to frolic at our bow. And then, just as we entered Puget Sound, death for the first time came underwater to the Nautilus to take one of the finest submarine sailors in the Navy, First Class Torpedoman Theodore Szarzynski, who died of a cerebral haemorrhage.

THIRTEEN

Pins and Needles

There were many things to occupy my mind en route to Seattle, but the one material problem I concentrated on was the leak in the condenser system. Our messages to Washington concerning it were written in reassuring tones, but the plain fact was that we had not stopped it.

Paul Early and I held several conferences a day, racking our minds for a solution. By the time we were a few hours out of Seattle, either we or the experts in San Francisco had explored every conceivable avenue. Yet each one had led to a dead end.

I thought of a Sunday afternoon conversation I had had years ago with my father-in-law, a research chemist for a large organization. Then an idea flashed into my mind. A ridiculous, improbable, crazy idea it was. But, I thought, we've tried everything else. Why not?

I called Paul Early into my stateroom.

"Paul," I said, "When we get to Seattle, I want you to send your men around town, in civilian clothes, to various gasoline stations. Let each man buy several cans of that stuff you pour into automobile radiators to stop leaks. What do they call it—Stop Leak?"

Early's lips curled into a faint smile. I could see that he could not tell whether I was serious or not.

"I'm serious, Paul," I said. "Let's get together about thirty gallons of the stuff. I think it comes in quart cans, so we'll need one heck of a lot of cans. But tell your men not to disclose that they are from the Nautilus. For more reasons than one, this has got to be done strictly under cover."

"Aye, aye, Captain," Early replied enthusiastically. He could see then that I was not joking.

"Now, when you get that stuff aboard, you know what to do. Pour it into the condenser system, just as you would into an automobile radiator. And get enough so we will have some extra for the trip."

Early detailed Chief Stuart Nelson to spearhead the Stop Leak project. After the ship had moored, half a dozen Nautilus sailors went ashore in civilian clothes, and I believe they must have bought every can of Stop Leak in Seattle. They brought 140 quart cans back to Nautilus, and under Early's supervision poured half of it into the condenser system. What a scene! A hundred-million-dollar nuclear-powered submarine, the most advanced ship in history, and Early's men pouring in $1.80 cans of Stop Leak. But for us it was no laughing matter. It was deadly serious business. We knew that the polar transit itself probably hung in the balance.

Incredible as it may seem, the Stop Leak treatment worked. Wherever it was, the leak was plugged. Neither in Seattle, nor later, would this problem arise again. Even as I write these words, the weak spot has yet to leak. It may be that some of the work we did earlier, or the expert combing in San Francisco helped or, perhaps, plugged the leak altogether. But you couldn't get a man on Nautilus to believe this. Today they are probably the most enthusiastic proponents of Stop Leak in the world.

Once we had docked in Seattle, I put into execution a plan I had long since tucked away in the back of my mind: a last-minute aerial reconnaissance of the ice conditions near the Bering Strait and Alaska. This, too, was done under cover. Five minutes after Nautilus berthed in Seattle, I slipped past the welcoming committee in civilian clothes and raced over the gangway, supposedly on emergency leave. I met Dr. Lyon, who would accompany me, at the Municipal Airport, where we had reservations on a commercial airliner leaving in a very few minutes for Alaska.

In preparation for this expedition, I had obtained special

identification papers. I travelled under the name of Charles A. Henderson, ostensibly a civilian technician attached to Lyon's outfit, the Naval Electronics Laboratory in San Diego. Since it was not unusual for Dr. Lyon to be seen in Alaska scrutinizing ice conditions, and since up to that point he had had no overt connection with the Nautilus, he used his own name. In Seattle, as we were climbing aboard the airliner, he said to me, "I thought things like this happened only in story books."

We flew to Fairbanks, where we stopped overnight, and then on to Nome where, roped in with the tourists, we toured the city in a bus and ate reindeer steak. From Nome we flew north to a small village, Kotzebue, where Dr. Lyon had made arrangements to charter a private plane, a single-engine Cessna 180, flown by a bush pilot named Ernie Cairns. Cairns was fussing around the engine of the plane when we arrived.

"I just checked her out a minute ago," he said. "I think I better work on this thing a little bit before we take off."

I agreed that the little grasshopper of an airplane looked as if it needed working on. As Lyon and I paced back and forth, I said, "Doc, the security of this operation will kill us yet—if we manage to stay out of jail long enough."

At last we were off, winging toward the Bering Strait, and thence toward the northernmost land possessed by the United States, Point Barrow. As far as Cairns knew, we were simply two scientists gathering data for a Navy scientific presentation. I posed as Lyon's assistant.

"I wonder if I can masquerade as well as Major Keating," I laughed to myself. He was no longer on board Nautilus; otherwise, I might have asked him for some pointers.

Zooming low over this bleak area in a single-engine plane, sometimes as far as fifty miles from land, my heart was frequently in my mouth. But Lyon and I were steadily compiling information. We noted many stretches of open water along our prospective route—an encouraging sign. All in all, we judged that conditions were not ideal, but probably worth risking a try.

Our brief air reconnaissance was not without its moments of drama. Toward the end of our mission, we unexpectedly ran critically short of fuel. Cairns radioed a nearby Air Force DEW Line station, reporting the emergency and requesting permission to land.

Back came the Air Force: "Who do you have on board?"

Cairns replied: "Two civilians."

Air Force: "Permission *not* granted to land."

Seeking an alternative solution, Cairns turned towards a small Eskimo village at Point Lay, Alaska, where he knew of a gasoline cache left there by the bush pilots against just such a predicament as ours. He dragged the small plane along a sandy beach, wheeled around and landed, only a few miles from the point where Will Rogers and Wiley Post ran out of fuel and crashed many years ago. The Cessna was filled with fuel, and then, with six Eskimos pushing on each wing to boost us out of the soft sand, Cairns jockeyed the plane into the air. Our wheels cleared a large and formidable log by inches.

We landed at Point Barrow on a slushy, half-frozen airstrip, debarked, and took the "limousine"—a covered truck that looked as though it might have first seen service on the front in World War I. The hotel at Barrow is a Quonset-hut type of building operated by, of all people, a school-teacher from Mississippi, who spends her summers there. I registered as Charles Henderson, and later we visited a local Eskimo establishment for a hamburger, which was quite expensive— $1.25—but good. Eskimos were sitting around, listening to a juke box and drinking coffee. When we finally turned in, it was about one o'clock in the morning, but still daylight. On Sunday, June 8, I was back aboard the Nautilus.

On my return I found that Captain Jack L. Kinsey (no relation to the late sex expert of the same name), a psychiatrist from the Polaris submarine project, had reported aboard. Dr. Kinsey, one of the few qualified submarine doctors in the Navy, was part of the cover operation plan. He would lend a measure of authenticity—within Navy circles—to the fact that we were actually going to make a long, submerged endurance run to gather data for the Polaris programme. Ostensibly, he would study the "problems" that arose when men were subjected to the stresses of long submerged cruises under unusual conditions. I learned later that when he first reported aboard one of the Chiefs said, "Well, Captain, you may have us on the couch at the start of this cruise, but before it is over we'll have you on the couch." Not having a couch on board, the matter was never fully resolved.

Many times in the past, well-meaning psychiatrists had come aboard Nautilus to study this or that. The crew has never been able to take these studies seriously. Once a psychiatrist came aboard carrying a small box with a hole into which Nautilus sailors were supposed to stick their index fingers. If the man's hands trembled slightly, the index finger would make contact with the side of the hole, and electronically a "score" would be run up. Every man was tested every day on the theory that the longer Nautilus remained submerged the more the hands would tremble. The sailors called his device "the shaky box".

One salty Chief Petty Officer who considered, like most of the sailors, that such tests were hogwash, deliberately trembled violently on the first day, running up the astronomical "score" of about 5,500 contacts. Then, on each succeeding day, he held his hand steadier, and his "score," defying all theories, gradually dropped. On the final day it registered near zero. They still tell that story on Nautilus. Invariably someone adds, "I'll bet that head-shrinker is still trying to figure out what hit him."

Another yarn they spin on Nautilus concerning a psychiatrist is the case of John Teixeira, a Leading Quartermaster, and a very fine sailor indeed. After the psychiatrist had squared away his gear and begun his "studies," Teixeira got a pack of Camel cigarettes and tied a long string to the package. Every time Teixeira saw the psychiatrist coming, or knew he would shortly cross his path, "Tex" would throw the pack of cigarettes on the deck and trail it behind him, occasionally turning to say, "Come on, Camel. Come on, Camel." At dinner-time, he would drag the pack of cigarettes into the Crew's Mess, and tie up the string to a "Camel hitching post". A crewman would say, "Tex, take that damned camel out of here during chowtime. He ruins my appetite." Another would flick imaginary fleas from the camel out of his dinner plate. Tex would finally give in and with a dejected look leave the table, dragging the cigarettes behind him, saying, "All right, you guys, I'll take my camel up to the Torpedo Room hitching post, but just wait till you need a ride to Cairo."

They say, on Nautilus, that the psychiatrist hastened over the gangway when the ship finally got into port. Neither he nor his report has been seen since.

With the Stop Leak loaded on board and Dr. Kinsey present, we were almost ready to get under way. It was that afternoon, Sunday, June 8, that I sat in my stateroom on pins and needles, waiting for the word from Washington which would tell us whether our voyage would be a routine trip or a polar transit. When the go-ahead came through, I faced only one final problem: how to get Dr. Lyon and his assistant, Rex Rowray, who were hiding out in a hotel in Tacoma, on board without their being noticed.

In Navy and scientific circles a submarine plus Dr. Waldo Lyon equals an Arctic cruise. I had planned to bring them over the gangway at the last second—until I received word that a Navy photographer would cover our sailing. If a picture of Lyon and Rowray scooting over the gangway were released, I knew the cat would inevitably be out of the bag. If I brought them aboard well in advance of departure, the crew and others would instantly guess our mission.

There was only one solution. My Exec mustered all hands in the Crew's Mess for "pre-under-way quarters". Even the topside watch was relieved by one of the officers. While the crew was being routinely briefed on the fictional trip to Panama, Lyon and Rowray scampered aboard on a pre-arranged signal. We rushed them into a Wardroom state-room and locked the door. Lieutenant Ken Carr remarked, "Captain, these are the first men in history to be shanghaied to go to the North Pole."

A minor material failure in our main turbine system delayed

our departure until midnight. Such breakdowns always seem to occur when our propulsion plant has been idle. On the Nautilus we believe in the dictum of the aviators, which is "To keep a plane in good shape, keep it flying." The repairs were made with little inconvenience to us. However, the confinement of our "hostages," Dr. Lyon and Rex Rowray, was considerably prolonged. Lieutenant Shep Jenks slipped them apples and oranges to stave off hunger pangs, and empty bottles for obvious reasons.

At 0024 on June 9, Paul Early reported, "Ready to get under way." Mooring lines were singled up. With a final look around, I said, "Take in all lines. All back two thirds."

Nautilus, at last, was ice pack bound.

FOURTEEN

Toward the Pole

As we slipped into the darkness of Puget Sound, I passed the word to Lieutenant Bob Kelsey on the main deck to paint over our gleaming white identifying numerals—571—on the bow and sail. Our orders were to remain undetected and, if detected, to conceal our identity. During the dark surface run out of Puget Sound, the grey covering paint could dry.

Now, at last, I could release our concealed passengers—Dr. Lyon and Rex Rowray. I said to their "custodian," Shep Jenks:

"Release the hostages."

This, I thought, marked the end of months of double talk and side-stepping. I made preparations to brief the crew. Many of them had already caught sight of Dr. Lyon and Rowray. With Arctic expert Lyon on board, they knew we were not headed for the equator and Panama. I picked up the public-address mike: "All hands. This is the Captain speaking. Our destination for this trip is Portland, England, via the North Pole. . . ."

The reaction of the crew was superb. Robert E. Simonini cracked: "Well, I knew there was some reason I saved those two British pound notes." Steward Harvey retorted: "You may be in good shape, but this is going to cost me fifty cents. I've still got two Panamanian quarters."

Williamson, a Quartermaster who had come on board at the last minute from Sargo to replace a Nautilus sailor transferred on emergency leave, remarked, "Now I know why they said, 'You go. You're single.'" However, I want to emphasize that these were lighthearted jokes. Nowhere on board was there any evidence of apprehension. A look around, an ear cocked to orders being given, repeated back, and executed precisely and smartly, was enough to indicate to anyone that Nautilus was ready. The reaction confirmed my long-held opinion that no better crew had ever taken a ship to sea.

The first two hours under way in Puget Sound we steamed at moderate speed so that the wet paint covering our bow numbers would not be washed away. Off Marrowstone Point, we built up to full speed, and the bow dug in, pushing a wall of water before us. Nautilus was designed to run submerged. On the surface, when we reach a certain speed, power is wasted pushing the bow wave. Submerged, there is no such phenomenon. The bow wave disappears, and we can run considerably faster. For this reason, among others, we much prefer to cruise below.

Daylight came early in Puget Sound. In the early morning light, the Officer of the Deck steered devious courses to keep well clear of merchant shipping. A submarine flying no colours and with no identifying numbers could cause some excitement. Finally, at 0900, clear of the Strait of Juan de Fuca, a few miles off Swiftsure Lightship, the Officer of the Deck sounded two rasping blasts on the klaxon and in less than a minute we slipped down into our true element underneath the sea. After a brief, routine check of our ballast trim, we increased our speed to more than twenty knots and descended to a cruising level several hundred feet below the surface.

The main objective lying before us—indeed, we thought, the most challenging and dangerous portion of our mission—was to penetrate the ice-choked, narrow, shallow Bering Strait, which for any kind of ship is probably the most hazardous body of water in the world. Two "doors" were available to us. One lay to the west, or Siberian side of St. Lawrence Island, which straddles the south end of the Strait like a kind of unwelcome mat. The other door lay to the east, or Alaskan side of St. Lawrence Island. For several reasons, long ago, we had decided to try the western approach first. On our Great Circle route, it was closer. Moreover, on the western side of the island the water is deeper, and we had read in an old pilot book that the menacing shore ice receded earlier in the year.

Between us and St. Lawrence Island, of course, lay the sweeping, rugged Aleutian Island chain, some seventeen hundred miles distant. After we submerged, Shep Jenks gave the course which would take us to the edge of this barrier. Then Lieutenant Bob Kelsey, the Diving Officer on watch, directed Planesmen Greenhill and Brigman to shift steering and depth control to "automatic," a system that controls Nautilus submerged much the same as the automatic pilot on an aeroplane. At last we were on our way, towards a route no sailor had travelled before.

Our first morning at sea was quiet. Many of the officers and crew had been without sleep for twenty-four hours—or more. Our busy schedule of visitors and exercises with West Coast anti-submarine units had been taxing. But with a group whose average age is slightly more than twenty-six, recovery time is fast. By afternoon, life on board Nautilus began to pick up. The Exec, Frank Adams, launched the first of a series of under-ice familiarization lectures for the crew, covering a few of the thousand and one details that would transform us into a smooth-running team by the time we entered the ice. There were special watches to be trained, detailed instructions to be issued, and a comprehensive data collection team to be organized in support of the paragraph of the operation order that directed us to collect extensive scientific data.

As we moved northward, we ascended from the deep only occasionally to poke up our periscopes, radio antennae, and snorkel. We confirmed our underwater navigation by occasional observations of the stars, received important official radio messages from the antennae, and revitalized our air supply with the snorkel. Although we are fully capable of operating completely independently of outside air for weeks at a time, I wished to conserve our oxygen banks for the long cruise across the Arctic Basin and subsequent high-speed voyages to England and home.

A nuclear-powered submarine is primarily a weapon of war. None the less, it is the most comfortable means of sea travel known to man. At our cruising depth there is absolutely no motion; the ship is as steady and level as an ordinary living-room. Even when the roughest storm imaginable is raging overhead, at a depth of 250 feet and below, the water is calm as a millpond. Our air conditioning maintains the atmosphere in all living compartments at an ideal level: temperature 72 degrees; relative humidity 50 per cent. Nautilus sailors actually dislike surfacing (except for liberty) because in this steady sea environment it is easy to lose one's sea legs after several days submerged. The only real shortcomings of our underwater living is the almost total lack of news from the outside world.

Movies are the high point of recreation on board the Nautilus. Ordinarily we load one film for each day we expect to be at sea. Each film is shown twice a day, first in the afternoon and then again after supper, so that every watch-stander can see it. On this trip we had thirty films on board. One of the first to be shown after leaving Seattle was a submarine movie, *Hell and High Water*. A line in this movie, in a curious coincidence, provoked a belly laugh from the salty audience: "Who would have thought six months ago I would be on a submarine headed for the Arctic. . . ?"

Since we are almost always completely out of touch with normal time, place, and circumstance, we have found from long experience submerged that it is best to establish a semblance of routine living when we are under way in our dark element. Shortly after leaving Puget Sound, we set our clocks ahead in two four-hour jumps to conform with Greenwich Mean Time. This meant that we would live by the same regular hours during the entire voyage. Our cooks were affected most by these abrupt initial changes. By the time they squared away supper, it was almost time for breakfast.

Crew watches were organized on a routine basis—four hours on, eight hours off. However, as a special precaution, I increased the number of officers on watch from two to three—a Diving Officer in the Control Room, a Conning Officer at the periscope station, and an Engineering Officer in the Manoeuvring Room. Meanwhile, Dr. Lyon and his assistant, Rex Rowray, began checking the complex array of sensitive ice-detection equipment which we had installed earlier in the spring, ostensibly for our publicized "ice exercises" with Skate and Halfbeak. Lyon found that the deep-water pressure had punctured one of the topside ice detectors, but this was of little concern to us because we had several others in reserve.

Two days out, during the early morning, our radio picked up a report that a severe storm lay ahead of our track. The storm was moving northward. It would not influence us, of course, in our comfortable submerged home, but we were vitally concerned about its effect on the ice conditions in the Bering Strait and beyond. However, it was much too late to investigate. We would have to take our chance.

The impact of our mission was still pronounced. Our talented cartoonist, William J. McNally, Jr., was already working on North Pole insignia to mark our historic transit. John Krawczyk, our ship's photographer, was busy clicking the shutter. That day I overheard Richard T. Murphy, a seaman cook who had been on board ten months, shooting the breeze with James A. Morley. In all earnestness, Murphy faced his shipmate squarely and said, "Morley, you know last year I was a nobody. Today I am on my way to the North Pole."

Nautilus in dry dock at New London, Connecticut.

Moored at Seattle before departing on the Arctic voyage.

Nautilus berthed in Pearl Harbour just prior to departure for the North Pole.

The unusual bow of Nautilus makes for great underwater speed and efficiency. The conventional submarine Greenling offers an interesting comparison.

FIFTEEN

A Closed Door

On the third day, when we left the comparatively warm Japanese current astern, the temperature dropped sharply. At cruising depth, our bathy-thermograph, with which we check the outside water tempera-ture, registered 39 degrees Fahrenheit.

Nautilus had not operated in water as cold as that for several months. During the morning we descended to our maximum, classified depth, to check for leaks. Sometimes fittings that are tight in warm water will leak with a fall of temperature. After checking all compartments by telephone, Imon L. Pilcher reported to Diving Officer Lieutenant Kelsey: "All compart-ments report no leaks." Confident of the tightness of the ship, I ordered a return to cruising depth.

On the fourth day, as we approached the Aleutian chain, the luxury of cruising in very deep water terminated. We gradually rose towards the surface, keeping a gimlet eye on the fathometer which recorded the rapidly decreasing depth of the water beneath us. For several days to come, we knew, we would have to navigate with great precision, threading our way through shallow, island-dotted waters. On the night of June 12, we made our initial landfall on Unimak Island, seventeen hundred miles north-west of Seattle.

With periscopes up, we gazed in wonderment at the rugged, snow-capped peaks and valleys of the Aleutian Islands. Manoeuvring slowly, seeking a northward channel through the island chain, Navigator Shep Jenks took one fix after the other. At length he was satisfied, and he aimed Nautilus for a fairly open stretch between two islands. Diving deep, we sped through.

By midnight we had threaded our first needle and had intro-duced Nautilus to yet another body of water, the Bering Sea.

We steered a steady submerged course, only occasionally taking a peek through the periscope. The bottom of the shallow Bering Sea is extraordinarily flat. Scientists say this is due to heavy layers of silt which have accumulated over thousands of years. The silt is deposited when pieces of landlocked ice, containing fragments of earth, break away, drift out to sea, and melt. We proceeded with caution, but what distracted me most in the Bering Sea was the topsy-turvy time element. By our clocks, the sun set at seven o'clock in the morning and rose at two in the afternoon. However, in our isolated, regu-lated world, it made little difference to the crew.

Shipboard activity progressed normally. In the cribbage tournament, which had been going full blast since our depart-ure, Gilbert Spurr, Engineman First Class, was eliminated at four thirty in the morning in the third game, by Lieutenant Ken Carr. The off-going watch relaxed over coffee and dough-nuts in the Crew's Mess before turning in for a few hours' sleep. In the Engine Room David H. Long, Engineman Second Class, tended the evaporators, which provide fresh water for showers, shaving, cooking, and the steam plant. "Plenty of water for all comers" was his posted motto. However, our supply of fresh fruits and vegetables—avidly consumed in our world of artificial light—was rapidly disappearing.

Never before had I seen such interest on the Nautilus in regard to the ship's position. It even surpassed the interest in the major-league baseball scores which we obtained, occa-sionally, when we could catch brief snatches of press radio broadcasts. A constant stream of crewmen peered over the Navigator's shoulder to examine the chart. Richard T. Bearden, Machinist's Mate First Class, and Norman A. Vitale, Engine-man First Class, were appointed "Engine Room navigators," and posted a large polar chart near the reactor plant controls. Every hour or so, they plotted Nautilus' position as she churned ever northward.

On Friday, June 13, four days out, skimming along barely

one hundred feet above the flat, featureless floor of the Bering Sea, we passed the Pribilof Islands. On the following day, we rose to snorkel depth to revitalize our air for the last time. From then on, I intended to make use of our normal air revitalization system: oxygen from stored bottles; machines to maintain such gases as carbon dioxide, carbon monoxide, and hydrogen well below harmful levels. Commander Dobbins, Nautilus' Medical Officer, and his two hospital corpsmen were assigned the responsibility for checking the concentration of dangerous gases in our sealed atmosphere.

Although our shipboard clocks read noon, it was evening topside when we completed our final ventilation. The sea had been very calm, but visibility was blotted out by a heavy fog that lay across the water. Pulling down our snorkel, we slipped deeper to make a final check of our magnetic compasses, which we would use if our electronic compasses and inertial navigator failed.

Approaching the western door at 2200 that evening, Siberia lay on our left and St. Lawrence Island on the right. Coming up to periscope depth for a navigational fix, we found the sky a beautiful, cloudless blue and the seas very calm. The snow-capped, bleak Siberian coast, some twenty miles distant, was clearly visible. In fact, due to a freak atmospheric condition we could actually see mountains on the Siberian coast a hundred miles away. But there was no time for sight-seeing. After the quick fix, we went deep, setting a course northward for the Bering Strait. Our route would keep us to the east of the International Boundary Line, laid down many years ago, and observed to this day by the United States and the U.S.S.R.

Late on the "night" of June 14, we encountered our first ice. It was detected initially on the electronic gear. Through the periscope we could see its shadow blotting out the rays of the sun. The ice was neither thick nor plentiful, yet we decreased our speed. Word soon spread through the ship, and many of the crewmen gathered at the electronic instruments to watch. For our new men, it was their first contact with ice, and they stared in fascination. The veterans of our last trip under the ice simply grunted: "Brash and block again," or "Just like last time." It *was* just like last time, with the exception that our movements were severely restricted in the shallow Bering Sea. We were sandwiched in by ice above and the flat bottom close below. Utmost care would be needed to keep from striking either.

By the time the watch changed, we were easing under floes forty yards across and twenty feet thick. After a hurried but careful survey, we estimated that heavy ice covered about 60 per cent of the water overhead. The percentage caused me considerable concern. At this comparatively low latitude, we had expected a far smaller figure. The sonar watch, manning all equipment, strained for accurate and continuous readings, since there was only forty-five feet of water between our keel and the ocean floor, and less than twenty-five feet from the top of our sail to the bottom of the ice.

At twenty minutes after midnight, near St. Lawrence Island, we passed beneath a huge block of ice which projected thirty feet below the surface of the water. To be frank, I was astonished. Dr. Lyon and I exchanged apprehensive glances.

When the polar ice pushes southward in winter-time against the walls of the Bering Strait funnel, layers of ice jam one atop another, pushing the ice ever deeper. This ice, which clings to the shore in winter, is called "rafted ice". In the warmer months, the polar pack itself recedes, leaving the rafted ice stuck to the shore. Gradually, this rafted ice breaks loose and floats out to sea.

The total thickness of ice which has spent its entire life in the open sea, such as the true polar pack, is fairly predictable. The thickness of rafted ice chunks that have broken away from the coastline is not. No one has made a complete study of rafted ice, but Dr. Lyon and I knew that chunks as thick as sixty feet had broken loose from the Alaskan coast. We knew nothing of the thickness of the rafted ice which had torn away from Siberia, the coast nearest us. Nothing—except that we had just squeezed under a monstrous piece of Siberian ice projecting thirty feet below the surface!

I thought of the even shallower stretches of water that lay before us. An unnerving question arose in my mind: what if we met a piece of Siberian shore-ice just ten feet thicker than the last one?

I conferred in private with Dr. Lyon, telling him that I was genuinely concerned about the ice picture. He replied, quietly, that he was, too. We had both learned that ice is an enemy to be respected, even at the cost of time. The year before, we had run into battle like an eager young fighter ready to whip the world and literally got both eyes blackened. This year I was determined to prevent any serious injury, no matter what the cost.

There was not much time to ponder the situation. Within a few seconds I had made up my mind, I approached the Conning Officer, Lieutenant Ken Carr, and in a soft, even voice, ordered him to reverse course. The western door was closed.

Our newspaper that day, entitled "The Panama-Arctic Shuffle," contained a remark that gave us all a chuckle:

Classified: Lieutenant Harvey wants to know if it is Russian or American ice that has been giving us trouble.

SIXTEEN

A Narrow Escape

With the western door locked, I intended to try the other, circling south around St. Lawrence Island, and then north off the coast of Alaska. We would pass over extremely shallow water in spots, which would force us to cruise part of the time with our sail, or perhaps the entire upper hull, exposed, thus increasing our chances of being detected. But we had no other choice.

By 0600 the following morning, we had completed our withdrawal from the Siberian ice. We ascended vertically to obtain a fix on St. Lawrence Island. There was little or no wind, and no ice in sight. However, at that moment, unexpectedly, the sonar reported ice off the bow. Incredulous, I wheeled the scope around. The "ice" turned out to be two seagulls bobbing in the water. It was reassuring to see how amazingly sensitive our ice detection gear could be. Later, with these instruments we picked up and tracked another bird, a diving cormorant.

By noon, when we again came to periscope depth to ventilate the boat, the weather was foggy, the visibility less than a thousand yards. We obtained one last fix on St. Lawrence Island and were on our way. As soon as possible I passed the word to the crew that I had decided to give up the western door and would try the Alaskan route. To a man, I'm sure, they shared my disappointment that we had not been able to drive straight through to deep Arctic seas on the first try. I also told them that we would be cruising through shoal water, and that we might run on the surface. Typical comment: "I hope it's not on my watch."

The crew was in good spirits, but the gnawing suspicion that all was not well returned to worry me. The leak had been stopped. There had been no further sign of fire. But new omens had come along to replace these. Our well-laid plan to enter the pack through the western door had backfired. The master gyrocompass, our most critical piece of navigating equipment, was behaving peculiarly.

We circled St. Lawrence Island to the east, and turned north following the Alaskan coast. The water was shoaling rapidly. We eased up to eighty-five feet. Even at that depth, the fathometers showed only forty-five feet of water beneath the keel. Later that evening we rose to sixty-five feet, the top of our sail just barely underwater. The Conning Officer, Paul Early, kept a continuous watch through the periscope. The water was too shallow to duck under anything. We would have to manoeuvre around. We were moving at painfully slow speed.

A series of minor crises suddenly befell us. First, the master gyrocompass failed completely. However, our initial reaction of concern soon gave way to one of confidence. With the compass out of commission, the small malfunction which we had not previously been able to detect now made itself clearly evident. Raymond McCoole, who would soon be promoted to Ensign, and his assistant, Roland L. Cave, went to work.

Not long after that, Paul Early sighted a mast on the horizon, almost dead ahead. I was called immediately. I rushed to the periscope, all the while hoping that our sail, which was now partly out of water, had not been sighted. My first impression on viewing the distant object was that it was a snorkling submarine. "But what was it doing in these deserted waters?" I thought. "Could it be Russian?"

We closed in on the target rapidly, prepared for any eventuality. But very soon we breathed more easily. The target turned out to be a drifting log with two projecting roots which made it appear very similar to a submarine with two periscopes extended. We were abreast of the mouth of the Yukon River and, as time passed, we spotted many such logs. Only a couple

of hours later we came upon one so close that there was no time
to retract the periscope, which struck the log a glancing blow.
Fortunately, no damage was done.

By early afternoon we had once again reached the high
latitude mark for the cruise. The weather was moderately
clear, sea temperature well above freezing, and no sign of ice.
The news that we might now proceed northward under far
more favourable conditions spread like wildfire among the
crew. Spirits rose.

Late in the afternoon the rugged features of King Island—
just south of the Bering Strait—loomed in our periscope cross
hairs. We turned west, reaching for deeper water, hoping to
traverse the radar-scanned Strait at periscope depth or more.
That evening, when Conning Officer Bill Lalor reported a few
chunks of ice, we zigged north, leaving the ice on our port
beam. Shortly afterwards, we saw a massive mile-wide floe
which protruded above the water several feet. We were now at
the entrance of the Bering Strait, gateway to the Chukchi
Sea and the Arctic beyond.

The newspaper continued, as usual, to pepper the officers,
the crew, and our equipment:

Overland. North American's N6A Inertial Navigator had us
going overland, across the north-west Cape of St. Lawrence.
Actually, it was a short cut. Only three miles across.

Matinée. Dr. Lyon remarked at the Father's Day matinée:
"Wonder what Dr. Kinsey's report of the crew will be now?"
You had better watch it, Doc (Lyon, that is), or Doc (Kinsey,
that is) will have the AMA after you.

Flash. Rank seems to mean a lot nowadays even among the
passengers. Even Rex Rowray has involuntarily given up his
rank. Can we find something for Dr. Lyon to do so Rex can get
some rest?

Shortly after midnight, June 17, we sighted the Diomede
Islands fifteen miles ahead—Big Diomede, Russian-owned, and
Little Diomede, American-owned—population, one Eskimo

village. Soon after, the Siberian and Alaskan coasts loomed up through the haze. We remained at periscope depth in those shallow and restricted waters. There was no ice in sight except a few chunks near the Siberian coast. The seas were running about four feet high with numerous whitecaps. Conditions appeared most favourable for an undetected transit through the narrow, radar-scanned gap.

Actually, our trip through the Strait was accomplished with unexpected ease. We ran at periscope depth, and at 0530 our bow sliced into the waters of the Chukchi Sea. Like the Bering Sea south of the Strait, the Chukchi is flat and shallow, varying between 105 and 170 feet. Four hundred miles north across the Chukchi lay the deep Arctic Basin. If we could reach the Basin without bumping up against deep-draft rafted ice, I knew we had it made.

We threaded our way northward, trying to keep in at least 135 feet of water. A few hours after entering the Chukchi, we sighted our first piece of ice, dead ahead, range five miles. It was a lone floe measuring about thirty by fifty feet, projecting some ten feet above the water. Its irregular shape suggested a sailing vessel. The sun reflected a multitude of light greens and blues from its surface. It was a captivating sight. However, we had learned the year before that ice is equal in strength to a poor grade of concrete, so we changed course to give the floe a wide berth. We soon spotted other floes. We zigged and zagged until, at 0925, it appeared that ice covered the horizon as far as one could see. There was no choice then—we had to submerge. I ordered a depth of 110 feet.

We cruised at moderate speed, passing under occasional floes and chunks. At longitude 168 degrees 39 minutes west we crossed the Arctic Circle. Once again all our crew members were entitled to be called Bluenoses, although, to tell the truth, it was pretty hard to visualize cold weather in our 72-degree home.

Our feeling of elation at having reached this significant position was soon brought up short. The waters began to shoal dangerously. Since ice reports had been sporadic, I decided to ease up and see if we could safely cruise on the surface. After carefully checking the ice detection gear, I ordered the "ice pick"—one of the radio antennae—raised. As we inched up, I watched the antenna through the periscope. If it bent over, it would be a certain indication of ice overhead and I would still have time to "pull the cork".

Ascending slowly, to our great fortune, we found clear water all around. I gave orders to keep the boat on the surface. Since we were far from land, the risk of being detected was small. In shallow, unknown waters like the Chukchi, we could actually make better speed on the surface, and I was anxious to recover the time we had lost in our fruitless probe of the western door.

Dodging an occasional floe, we logged ninety miles in seven hours. Finally, at latitude 68 degrees 30 minutes north, the Conning Officer reported that the horizon was completely covered with ice. After a brief surveillance of this vast, seemingly endless ice barrier, we concluded that it was the long-sought, supposedly predictable polar pack itself. Relieved, and ringing with enthusiasm, Nautilus submerged to creep beneath it. At that time we did not expect to see daylight or open water again until we rose on the other side of the world near Greenland.

At first everything went smoothly. Ice covered only about 5 per cent of the surface and this was unerringly picked up by our supersensitive sonars. Some of the larger chunks had keels down to twenty feet—fifty feet above the top of our sail. Beneath the keel we had a good forty feet of water. To most submarine sailors this might be considered close quarters, but with our previous ice experience on the Nautilus we were not overconcerned. In fact, we felt safe in increasing speed to eight knots. But every man was alert at his station.

After an hour or so of watching the topside sonar recorder-pen trace the underside contour of the ice, I was convinced that we were indeed clear of the unpredictable shore ice and were well under the polar pack. We had travelled some 1,383 miles under this type of ice in our 1957 cruise and we knew it well. I authorized the Conning Officer to boost our speed to ten knots. Then I strolled down to the Crew's Mess to watch the movie, ironically titled *Hot Blood*.

In a very few minutes the long hours of tension began to tell. I returned to my cabin, lay down, and dozed.

At 2300, Tuesday, June 17—eight days out of Seattle—my doze was interrupted by the calm but emphatic words of Lieutenant Bill Lalor crackling from my cabin speaker. "Captain. Will you come in, please?" I hurried to the Control Room.

When I arrived, Bill reported matter-of-factly that Nautilus had just cruised under ice sixty-three feet thick! The ink tracing showed that the ice had passed only eight feet above the sail. I quickly ordered a swing to the left and a depth increase to 140 feet, a manoeuvre that would bring us to within twenty feet of the ocean floor. While we were turning, Alfred Charette, Sonarman First Class, quietly reported two massive ridges of ice lying directly ahead. Nautilus was almost under the first of the ridges.

I ordered speed slackened to dead slow. Our sonar revealed that the gigantic block under which we hovered was over a mile wide. Not in many years had I felt so uneasy in a submarine. Obviously, it was urgent that we move away from that ice. Fighting to keep an even tone in my voice, I again ordered the rudder put hard over.

As we crept into our turn, the recording pen wavered downward. All of us—Rex Rowray, who was operating the equipment; Bill Lalor, who was co-ordinating and checking on the ship's course, speed, and depth, together with sonar reports; and myself—stared transfixed. Then slowly the pen receded. We all breathed more easily. We had cleared the monstrous hunk by twenty-five feet.

But we were still in trouble. Our instruments told us an even more formidable barrier lay just ahead. I stared in disbelief at its picture on sonar. The books said this couldn't happen!

Slowly—very slowly—we moved forward. My eyes were

glued to the recording pen. Downward it swooped again—down, down, down. I reflexed, as if to pull my head into my shoulders. How I wished I could do the same with Nautilus! The small boy trying to squirm beneath the fence would soon be stuck. The inevitable consequences could be severe damage to our ship—perhaps even slow death for those on board.

I waited for, and honestly expected, the shudder and jar of steel against solid ice. The recording pen was so close to the reference line which indicated the top of our sail that they were, for what seemed like hours, almost one and the same. I—and others in the Attack Centre, I am certain—turned for assistance to the only Person who could help us.

In pure agony we stood rigidly at our stations. No man moved or spoke. Then suddenly the pen, which had been virtually stationary, slowly moved upward. The gap between the ice and Nautilus was widening. We had made it! We had cleared—by an incredible five feet—a mass of ice big enough to supply a hundred-pound block to every man, woman, and child in the United States.

It took only a second's reflection for me to realize that Operation SUNSHINE had already totally and irrevocably failed. Not even Nautilus could fight that kind of ice and hope to win. To the north of us lay many miles of even shallower water and possibly even deeper ice. There was no question about it. The only sane course was south. Reluctantly I announced my decision to the crew. I told them we would leave the pack, send off a radio report to the Chief of Naval Operations, Admiral Burke, and ask for further instructions.

I spent a long time drafting that message. After so many months of anxiety it was heartbreaking to have to report that our first probes had showed that we could not get through. It was clear that we would have to stand off and take a long look. I tried to make the report to the point, adding my firm belief that the operation would probably be feasible later on—after the ice boundary had receded to deeper water. And we needed more information. The world about us—the darkness below the ice—was as unmeasured as the far side of the moon.

Toward midnight, Rex Rowray came into the Wardroom for a cup of coffee. He joked about how much he had aged watching the ice recorder for those few tense minutes. I told him I had aged a great deal, too, and I had, literally. It was my thirty-seventh birthday.

SEVENTEEN

A Painful Retreat

We continued south, making a painful retreat toward the Bering Strait. Gradually the ice cover began to thin out. Occasionally we detected chunks extending below the water twenty to thirty feet. But we saw none resembling the monstrous mass that had blocked our route to the Arctic Basin.

On Wednesday, June 18, nine days out of Seattle, all sonars reported clear water overhead and we made a vertical ascent to periscope depth. I raised number two periscope slowly. Swinging the scope around, observing the bleak, choppy sea above, I said:

"All clear. No close ice in sight. Control, Conn . . . raise the port whip. Radio, transmit the message to CNO."

The "port whip" was our radio antennae. Within seconds a Navy radio operator at Pearl Harbour flashed back an abbreviated signal meaning, "I read you loud and clear. Transmit your message." Radioman Harry Thomas, surprised at the rapid response (radio transmission conditions in the Arctic area are notoriously bad), shifted his right hand to the telegraph key and proceeded with a rhythmic splatter of dots and dashes. In a very few minutes, I reflected sadly, my report would be in the Pentagon.

Visibility was good that morning. A twenty-knot wind whipped the four-foot waves, and small white-caps tumbled helter-skelter. Since the water was ice-free, I decided to run at periscope depth, with the radio antennae extended, to await further instructions from CNO. To maintain our oxygen supply we shut off the tanks. To conserve precious nuclear fuel, I granted permission to Paul Early to secure the port main turbine and run on one shaft. When we are just milling around, this saves us an appreciable amount of fuel at no cost in speed.

Soon, however, we were again face to face with an endless horizon of ice. We were puzzled because, on the trip north, this section of the Chukchi Sea had been clear. Apparently a fresh south-westerly breeze had shifted the ice eastward across our track. We pulled down our whip and periscopes, and then I gave the order to submerge. Under normal circumstances— that is, in deep water—this would have been by far the preferable and faster mode of travel. However, in our shallow sea, we were forced to inch our way along, dodging the heavier floes which lay in our path. It was exceptionally tedious cruising.

In late afternoon we came upon a very shallow stretch which we knew extended some forty miles along our route. On our trip up, it had been clear. Now it was covered by a mass of deep-draft, rafted Siberian ice. We found an open hole and I surfaced to look the situation over. It was immediately apparent that the only practical route lay beneath the ice. We were boxed in on three sides, and it might be days before conditions would permit surface, or periscope-depth, navigation.

I directed the Officer of the Deck, Paul Early, to twist the ship around to a northerly heading, toward clear water. We submerged slowly, descended to cruising depth, and then swung south, probing for the deepest troughs on the bottom. Soon we were negotiating the ice field, literally sandwiched in between ice and mud, with only a few feet to spare. When our sonar reported heavy masses of ice lying ahead, the Conning Officers, Lieutenants Lalor and Carr, would weave around, skirting anything of deep draft. We changed our cruising depth by inches, taking advantage of the slightest depression in the ocean floor. Reports from the fathometer were delivered with the regularity of an auctioneer's chant. Our track, laid out on a chart, resembled forty miles of crude mountain road, with sharp zigzagging and hairpin turns. This was classic submarine manoeuvring!

After several hours, the depth of the water began to increase gradually. When we arrived at a point where our fathometer registered 120 feet, Navigator Shep Jenks chortled: "Captain, we've just crossed into Jenks' Deep." Jokingly I assured him that I would petition the Navy Hydrographic Office to name that "extremely deep" region in his honour.

About midnight we reached an open stretch of water. I brought the ship up and we poked our whip out of the water to check for an answer to our message to CNO. It was, as I had hoped, on the "schedule" then being broadcast. Electrician's Mate Morley, glancing over the Radioman's shoulder, reported to one of the seamen: "Either it's in code or I have a limited vocabulary. I can't read a word of it."

The message was indeed in code and it was classified Top Secret. In essence, it said:

"I concur entirely with your prudent action in withdrawing from the ice pack. It is obvious that you have made a maximum effort. I tentatively concur with your recommendation to lay over at Pearl Harbour until conditions improve. Set course and stand by for further instructions. Remain undetected." It was signed "Arleigh Burke".

We continued south through the Chukchi, skirted a hundred miles of ice, traversed the Bering Strait, and entered the shallow Bering Sea. On June 20 we reached open water. From there the trip to Pearl was routine, with one exception—the elaborate programme to preserve the Top Secret security of SUNSHINE.

No detail could be overlooked. In giving the crew their instructions, I issued the first Top Secret order of my career. It stated that no facet of Operation SUNSHINE could be discussed with any person on board or ashore by either oral or written means. Private conversations on board concerning it were authorized, but only with the Commanding and Executive Officers.

All hands were ordered to search through their personal belongings and seal up in envelopes labelled Top Secret, all

(*above left*) Bathing at sea, which is made possible by flooding the stern slightly to let swimmers climb on and off with ease.

(*above centre*) Fairway Rock in the Bering Strait as seen through the periscope.

(*above right*) Commander Anderson looking over navigation charts with the navigator, Lieutenant Shepherd Jenks.

(*left*) On the bridge during the search for a place deep enough to dive safely under the ice.

Torpedoman making a routine check of the torpedo tubes as the ship
speeds beneath the Arctic ice.

letters, papers, notes, and charts—anything indicative of the operation. These would be locked up for an indefinite period of time under rigid custody. The same was true of all official ship's logs, charts, records, and reports, and even of a pair of fur-lined bedroom slippers I had bought at an Eskimo store in Alaska for my three-year-old son, Bill. When all this had been gathered and stored, our triple-lock safes were bulging.

Our security precautions also provided some laughs for the crew—badly needed after our harrowing experience in the polar pack. One of the men had stencilled two shirts with our North Pole insignia, designed by the ship's cartoonist, McNally. When the shirts were turned in, the owner commented: "This is the first time in history a shirt has become Top Secret." Because beards are somewhat indicative of cold-weather cruises, I ordered that all should be shaved off. One man asked Chief Torpedoman Larch, our Chief of the Boat, if he could keep the remnants of his beard by sealing it in a Top Secret envelope.

All our special Arctic gear, including cold-weather clothing, was hidden away. As we approached Pearl Harbour I conceived a cover operation to explain why we had not gone to Panama, and to justify our absence: a fictional southern cruise near the equator. I prominently displayed a chart tracing our imaginary voyage, and wrote a brief article so that all hands would have the same story.

It concluded:

> It was a routine cruise—material problems were few and atmosphere control was the best experienced to date. Elaborate plans were made for the first Equator-crossing by a nuclear-powered ship. However, on 20 June, still considerably north of the Equator, the ship received the change-in-operation order diverting us to Pearl. Failure to cross the Equator at this time and the prospective delay in getting home are naturally disappointing; however, the visit to Hawaii will add another interesting chapter to the voyages of the most travelled submarine in history.

A day out of Pearl Harbour, by radio dispatch, I was advised of plans to fly me to Washington and New London to brief CNO and Commander, Submarines, Atlantic, Admiral Warder, on our disappointing operation. A naval aircraft was placed at my disposal, and since there was extra room, I also requested permission to take along as many of the married officers and crewmen as we could get aboard. Through the thoughtful efforts of Admiral H. G. Hopwood, Commander of the Pacific Fleet, and Admiral E. W. Grenfell, boss of Pacific submarines, twenty-six officers and men would make the quick trip with me. One of them later cracked: "Captain, that's the first time I've flown eleven thousand miles round trip for a seventy-two-hour liberty."

We were clipping along, submerged, still a couple of hundred miles from Pearl when I again ordered the whip antennae extended. Over voice radio, I asked for the commercial over-seas operator. She answered at once, and within a couple of minutes she had got through to Mystic, Connecticut. In another minute Bonny was on the other end of the line.

"Hello," I said. "We're submerged one day out of Pearl. Has anyone told you that we're coming in here?"

"Yes," she replied excitedly. "Admiral Warder just called." And then laughingly, "I have already started packing my bags."

Both Bonny and I had many fine memories of Pearl Harbour, from the days when I was stationed there as skipper of the Wahoo.

"Well, hold on," I said. "I'm flying to Washington, and then I have to go up to New London. How about meeting me in Washington and we'll go up to New London together? Then you can fly back out here with me."

She agreed to that and said she would pass the word to the other wives that all were well on the Nautilus. I rang off, marvelling at the manner in which communications have shrunken the world.

In the early morning hours of June 28, we glided along through the tropical depths past Diamond Head and then headed south-west—away from land—to merge our position with an imaginary Nautilus approaching Pearl Harbour from just north of the equator. At six in the morning we joined our fictional sister and swung north toward the entrance of Pearl Harbour. I tried to put myself in a frame of mind of one returning from a southern voyage. It was obvious that all on board were trying hard to do the same.

We ascended to periscope depth. Through the periscope cross hairs I could see sparkling Oahu, a breath-taking sight. Seconds later Nautilus rose silently to the surface. A deck party under Chief Larch climbed topside to restore our identifying numbers. They reported the superstructure in surprisingly good condition considering that we had just completed six thousand miles of submerged running.

As we entered Pearl Harbour, exactly on schedule, a small boat eased alongside to embark Admiral Hopwood and Admiral Grenfell. The presence of these two officers on Nautilus and the welcome they had arranged was a humbling and impressive experience.

By the time we reached the inner harbour, a huge flower lei, thirty feet long, had been draped around our bow. Helicopters hovered overhead showering the decks and the water around us with thousands of orchids. Every ship in the harbour sounded prolonged blasts on their steam and air whistles. Fire boats and tugs sprayed water plumes high into the air. Hundreds, if not thousands, of people collected on the sea walls and piers to view and greet the world's first nuclear-powered ship. At our berth at the Submarine Base, a Navy band played "Anchors Aweigh," and four lovely Island girls danced the traditional hula. As someone later put it, "The only way Hawaii's aloha to the Nautilus could have been improved was to have the tugboats shoot up coloured water." Everyone on Nautilus was deeply moved.

At precisely 1000 Quartermaster Seaman Yuill noted in his log: "Moored port side to berth Sierra One, U.S. Submarine Base, Pearl Harbour." Dr. Lyon and Rex Rowray were kept under cover. Four hours after our arrival, we were airborne in a Navy transport, along with other Nautilus men, headed for Washington. There I met Bonny, and after briefing officers in the Pentagon, we flew to New London. Finally, at home, I had a moment's rest and relaxation.

My sons, Mike and Bill, each appeared taller by a full three inches. Mystic seaport was in full swing with the summer crowd, the backyard tomato plants were doing well, and Mike's sixteen-foot runabout had a loose steering cable. In these familiar, friendly surroundings, the unfamiliar, inhospitable Arctic seemed a million miles away.

EIGHTEEN

"The Reluctant Dragon"

In the Pentagon I briefed a handful of senior officers on Phase I of Operation SUNSHINE, stating with strong conviction my belief that another try should be scheduled for late July.

I knew we would need something more than a crystal ball to tell us what we needed to know about ice conditions, so I proposed a detailed and continuous series of aerial ice reconnaissance flights over our intended route in the Chukchi Sea, not in a Cessna 180, but in full-fledged, long-range naval aircraft. My bosses agreed, but once again the complicating factor was security. It was absolutely necessary that the flights be programmed and conducted without the people involved being aware of their purpose. This would not be easy.

After considering several possible solutions with the officer in the Pentagon who had lived, breathed—indeed, devoted almost every minute of his time to Operation SUNSHINE— Commander Duke Bayne, we decided the best way would be to send a Nautilus officer to Alaska to co-ordinate and arrange the whole show. Admirals Combs and Daspit quickly approved our proposal.

I considered returning to Alaska myself, but I did not want to be away from the ship for so long a period. There were many material items I wanted to oversee personally during the layover in Pearl Harbour. Thus it was that I chose my Navigator, Shep Jenks, for this all-important, high-level mission. I knew he could handle the job. Moreover, with him it would be an easy matter to launch the operation because he was at that time one of the small group from Nautilus on leave in New London.

Realizing that he would be leaving in a few hours for the return flight to Pearl, I grabbed a telephone. "Shep. My apologies to Barbara for making you stay around the house, and I can't tell you why, but hold fast in New London. I'll see you to-morrow night."

Next evening in my backyard at Mystic, I laid out the plan to Jenks. He grasped the concept immediately.

The "cover" for Jenks was as follows: He would go to Washington immediately and be transformed from a Nautilus officer to a Pentagon type, a special representative of OP-33, a branch of the Chief of Naval Operations. He would study the inner workings of the Pentagon and lose his identity as a sub-marine officer. He would learn the names of his temporary bosses and know how they fitted into the over-all organization of the Pentagon. He would be simply a Pentagon naval officer concerned with planning Arctic and Antarctic operations. And, as such, he would go to Alaska to study ice conditions in the Chukchi.

Through Rear Admiral Warder in New London, Jenks was issued a set of orders which made no mention of Nautilus or any other submarine organization. His wife, I am sure, was completely baffled during the following three days. Studying the task ahead, Jenks pulled himself into a shell, telling his wife that he would go to Washington for a period and then rejoin Nautilus just before she sailed from Pearl. He added to the mystery, no doubt, when he told her he would probably not have time to write and that it would be impossible for her to contact him. Barbara, however, asked no questions.

At 0900 on July 7, Jenks reported in the Pentagon to Duke Bayne. Within five rather hectic hours he had been briefed on Pentagon organization, and met his new "boss," Captain Harold S. Hamlin, Jr., a representative of OP-33. Soon he was headed for the airport with "open ticket" orders, which stated, among other things: "You are authorized to omit any of the above-mentioned places and to vary the above itinerary as may be deemed necessary." As he drove along, Jenks noted that the operator of the motor-pool car was a submarine sailor,

Engineman First Class William Packett, on shore duty. Jenks said later, "I wondered what Packett would say if he knew that he was participating that very moment in Operation SUN-SHINE."

Thirty-seven hours and four thousand miles later, Jenks arrived in Alaska. In his pocket was a letter of introduction from Admiral Combs to Rear Admiral A. W. McKechnie, Commander, Alaskan Sea Frontier, authorizing Jenks to reveal to Admiral McKechnie all details of Operation SUN-SHINE. By the time he arrived at the Admiral's office, Jenks had removed his dolphins from his uniform and all cards from his wallet which might connect him with submarines or the Nautilus. His cigarette lighter, bearing Nautilus insignia, and tie clasp with a similar decoration, were in his bureau drawer in Connecticut. He had withdrawn money from his own savings account to buy food and cigarettes.

When Jenks sat down to brief the Admiral on the purpose of his trip, the Admiral's Chief of Staff, Captain G. D. Roullard, was present. Jenks, embarrassed, turned to the Captain. "Sir, I am sorry, but I am authorized to reveal the information I have only to the Admiral." Captain Roullard graciously excused himself.

When Jenks completed his briefing on Operation SUNSHINE, and had laid out his requirements for aerial ice reconnaissance, the Admiral called in several members of his staff to set up the details. They knew only that Jenks was from OP-33, and that he had been sent to Alaska on a special mission by Admiral Combs, and that Admiral McKechnie had directed that all men under his command provide assistance. As Jenks later put it: "The spirit of co-operation shown by Admiral Mc-Kechnie was the prime factor in enabling me to get the information we needed to get Nautilus through the ice-covered water in the shallow Chukchi."

These preparations were not easy. Many of McKechnie's staff, working in the dark, could not understand why Jenks wanted certain details, nor could they understand why CNO had sent a special representative in place of the usual written request for information. Jenks kept saying over and over: "I don't know why Admiral Combs wants it this way. All I know is that I was called in, briefed on the exact details of what to do, and was sent off to do it." Consumed with curiosity, McKechnie's staff co-operated fully, and by the following day flight schedules and plans had been worked out to Jenks' satisfaction.

That evening Jenks reported for duty with Commander, Patrol Squadron Nine, no doubt the first submariner ever to be attached to the unit. By Thursday, July 10, he reached Eielson Air Force Base in Fairbanks, Alaska, where Navy P2V patrol planes were stationed. The P2V, ironically, is an anti-submarine plane. That day he made the first of the patrol flights covering Nautilus' future track.

Jenks was well equipped for the ride. Squadron Nine had issued him special cold-weather survival equipment, including an immersion suit, in case they had to ditch in the frigid water. He carried survival gear in the pockets of his flying suit, a garment that must have made Jenks appear somewhat ridiculous. It was a size 30 short. Lanky Jenks wears a 34 long! Over all of this, he fastened a Mae West and a parachute harness. Jenks later said: "All these things were good for the morale of a submariner out of his element. But I kept thinking of that poster on Nautilus which says 'Evil, Evil, Man Was Never Meant to Fly'. "

Fly Jenks did, day in and day out. Although puzzled, the pilots in Squadron Nine took Jenks any place he asked, all the while muttering, "This guy has more pull around here than the Admiral." At the end of each flight, he filled out a report which was routinely forwarded to Pearl Harbour. But from Admiral Hopwood's office it was hand-delivered to Admiral Grenfell who had it hand-delivered to me. Jenks' reports indicated that the ice was steadily receding, but that it would be many days before we could get under way.

One day the Commanding Officer of Squadron Nine, Commander R. F. Peterson, who had been away when Jenks came on board, flew in. Naturally curious, he talked at great length with Jenks. Peterson had recently completed a tour of duty in another section of the Pentagon known as OP-44. Later Jenks reported: "When he asked me for details on the organization and specific questions about certain branches of the Pentagon, all I could do was plead ignorance, saying I had only been in the Pentagon a couple of months. He must have thought I was a complete ignoramus. I did my best to avoid him from then on."

One day, while flying over the ice, a low fog obscured the rugged pack boundary. Jenks called the cockpit from his observation station in the plastic nose of the plane and asked the pilot to go down close to the ice. As Jenks told me later, "It was my own fault for asking. The co-pilot, Bill Bell, took the plane down to fifty feet. I thought he would never pull out of the dive. To see the ice go by that close at some two hundred miles an hour convinced me more than ever that I am a submariner."

In the evenings, inevitably, there were bull sessions, during which, quite naturally, these aggressive anti-submarine pilots boasted of their triumphs over submarines in war exercises. For Jenks, who knew the other side of the story, but could not defend it, this was the most trying time of all. One evening Commander Peterson remarked, "All this ice reconnaissance is fine, but we'd much prefer to be anti-submarining." Swallowing hard, Jenks laughed to himself: "I wonder what he will think when he finds out he has been pro-submarining."

With a mass of data compiled, and arrangements made for the ice reconnaissance to continue according to our needs, Jenks called Washington and got permission to return to Nautilus in Pearl Harbour. On leaving Alaska, Jenks bought an Eskimo doll as a souvenir for his daughter Deborah, age two. When he came on board Nautilus, having travelled over fourteen thousand miles in eleven days, the doll was immediately classified Top Secret and locked in the three-combination safe.

I, and the other Nautilus men who had made the quick air trip to the States, had long since returned to Pearl Harbour.

Bonny, determined not to miss a chance for a visit to Pearl, had arrived by commercial airliner. Admiral Grenfell had turned over his special quarters in the BOQ to Bonny and me, and we were quite comfortable. In the evenings we got away to visit some old haunts and re-live old memories, but to tell the truth, I did not see as much of Bonny as I wished. On Nautilus, we were busy returning Hawaiian hospitality, by conducting tours of the ship for military and civilian personnel —some three thousand—and by taking Naval personnel— over two hundred—on brief trips out to sea. In between times, we were working over our gear and studying conditions far to the north.

I was most anxious to install emergency breathing apparatus for the remaining two-thirds of the crew, so that if a fire broke out, not only the ship, but all hands could be saved. When I presented this request to Admiral Grenfell, he moved into action immediately, and within a very short time face masks and air supplies had been provided for every officer and crewman on Nautilus. During one of our brief trips to sea, we conducted several drills which required the crewmen to don the face masks. When I asked for crew reaction, one man piped up: "They're fine, Captain, but it's sure hard as hell to drink a cup of coffee with one of 'em on." I have been told that this emergency breathing apparatus will become standard equipment on all nuclear-powered submarines.

Another new item installed on Nautilus in Pearl Harbour was a closed-circuit television set with the transmitter, or lens, mounted topside facing up. In theory, this system would give us a constant visual picture of the ice, far better than we could get through the periscope. It would be most helpful in locating leads or polynias in the ice if it became necessary, or if we wanted to come to the surface. After the gear had been hooked up, one admiral cracked: "You know, Anderson, that gadget is going to save the Navy several million dollars a year."

"In what way, Admiral?" I asked. I was genuinely puzzled.

"Well, instead of pulling these big ships into dry dock all the time to inspect their bottoms, we'll just send you and your TV set beneath them and let you do the inspecting."

Meanwhile, we observed from Admiral McKechnie's ice reports that conditions were rapidly becoming favourable for a second attempt to reach the Arctic Basin. We set our departure date for July 21. Still another cover operation plan had to be devised to justify our absence for the second trip. Reviving a familiar theme, Admiral Grenfell announced that Nautilus would make a submerged endurance run from Pearl Harbour to Panama.

All during our stay in Pearl Harbour, my men, and the men in the repair shop at the Submarine Base, had been working day and night on the Mark 19 gyrocompass which had failed near the Bering Strait on the first probe. At first we thought we had licked the trouble, but in our operations in and out of Pearl Harbour we noted that the compass was becoming increasingly erratic. Beneath the ice our compass, especially the Mark 19, would be our most vital piece of equipment. I was determined that it be in perfect condition before attempting another polar crossing.

As our proposed day of departure neared, I became concerned. Our compass experts were not making much progress. I called Washington and asked them to send a Sperry gyrocompass expert to Pearl Harbour by the fastest possible means. Awaiting his arrival, we postponed our sailing time by one day. The submarine staff officers at Pearl Harbour, unaware of our real destination, could not understand all the fuss over one simple erratic compass. Said one: "You people have three other compasses. What are you worried about?" Swallowing my pride, I replied: "Well, that's right. But on Nautilus we don't believe in getting under way unless everything is working properly." After that, the submariners at Pearl Harbour jokingly began calling Nautilus "The Reluctant Dragon."

The engineer from Sperry, a very bright and knowing expert, quickly found the source of trouble in the Mark 19, and within a short time corrected it. I was so impressed by his ability that I asked him to go along on the trip—supposedly to Panama—to make sure the compass remained in perfect working condition. He begged off. He and his wife were about to adopt a small child, and he wanted to get home as quickly as possible.

At long last, we were ready to head north again. I bade farewell to Bonny, who returned to the States, then paid my respects to Admiral Grenfell, whose organization at Pearl Harbour had given us such fine support and backing. At that time Admiral Grenfell bestowed on Nautilus a simple but eloquent compliment. "I certainly will be glad when I have a nuclear-powered submarine in my command," he said.

As we made last-minute preparations to get under way, I reflected on one aspect of Operation SUNSHINE, one that indicates the remarkable loyalty and competence of the crew. For almost four weeks 116 men of the Nautilus had been in Pearl Harbour. Many had been home on short leave. The temptation to talk about our first, unsuccessful try at crossing the polar ice must have, at times, been overwhelming. Even though we had failed on our mission, it was, nevertheless, a stirring and dramatic sea story. Yet not a word had leaked and Dr. Lyon, with a new assistant, Mr. Archie Walker, were sneaked aboard.

There were many amusing and, as usual, absurd, incidents caused by the high security during those four weeks. My favourite was the story told by a Chief Petty Officer, one of those who made the aeroplane trip to New London. Not knowing, of course, when we originally left New London in April that we might wind up in England, the Chief had taken only khaki uniforms on the first voyage. Aware that if our second attempt proved successful we would dock in England, he was very anxious to return to Nautilus with a set of blue uniforms, which would be required there.

One morning he said casually to his wife, "I think I'll take a set of blues back with me. Where are they?"

"They're stored away. But what in the world do you want with blues in Hawaii and Panama?"

The Chief, hemming and hawing, making this excuse and

that, finally said, "Well, who knows when a man will need blues for a special ceremony or something?"

The Chief's wife, wise in the ways of the Navy, replied: "It's ridiculous. There's no point to it. You just leave the blues where they are."

Realizing that if he pressed the matter further, his wife might put two and two together, the Chief reluctantly gave in and returned to Nautilus—minus his blues.

As we cast off all lines and backed out of our slip at Pearl Harbour, I recalled that story. Thinking of the dark unknown that lay ahead, I said to myself, "I wonder if he will need those blues after all."

NINETEEN

Record Run North

Nautilus slipped silently through the calm waters of Pearl Harbour. Darkness had fallen. The deck gang quickly painted over our identifying numbers. The large party of submariners who had bid us aloha had returned to their homes. Admiral Grenfell, who was among them, had given us an encouraging farewell message. Our Queen of the Seas was under way for her third polar voyage.

Few people realize the beehive of activity that goes on aboard a nuclear submarine at dockside between cruises. Mail arrives by the bagful. Official letters and reports are sent off in huge stacks. Machinery is overhauled. New equipment is installed. Literally hundreds of man-hours are consumed in loading supplies—torpedoes, oxygen, spare parts, and medical supplies, not to mention coffee, steaks, hot chili peppers, rags, transistors, beans, hydrogen, acetylene, nitrogen, freon, carbon-dioxide (for the Coke machine), ball bearings, soap, torpedo alcohol, two dozen different grades of oil and grease, film, paper, typewriters, radishes, aspirin, and so on ad infinitum.

Old hands are transferred; new faces appear. The period at Pearl Harbour was no exception. Lieutenant Tonseth was transferred to Nuclear Power School in New London; Lieutenant Fears to a new atomic-powered submarine, the Triton. Chief McCoole was commissioned an Ensign and reported for indoctrination into the mysteries of being a naval officer at Newport. Chief Yeoman James went back to New London to work for Nautilus' first skipper, Captain Wilkinson. Lieutenants Hall and Kassel, recent graduates of the nuclear training programme, reported aboard Nautilus for duty, as did Seamen

Fowlks and Hall and Fireman King. Clemente Ortega, Yeoman Second Class, came in from New London to replace Yeoman James.

It is always a relief to get to sea.

When we cleared the entrance channel, I called for full speed. As the ship surged forward, I realized that the electric excitement of our Seattle departure had been replaced by solid, calm, matter-of-fact determination. Now wiser, more experienced, and better in tune with the frozen elements ahead, we would, God willing, succeed.

Three minutes past midnight, Wednesday, July 23, with our clocks set on Seattle time (we did not, as before, tempt fate by setting them in advance to England's time), we nosed into the deep water south of Oahu and levelled off at cruising depth. I noted that all our machinery, including the compasses and the complex inertial navigator, was working perfectly. To my great satisfaction, our sonar operators reported porpoises frolicking close aboard. With that news, I was sure then that our cruise would be a success.

Making over twenty knots, we soon rounded Oahu through the Kauai Channel and again set course for Yunaska Pass in the Aleutian chain. We would penetrate the Bering Strait through the closer western door, which we knew was then free of ice. This was to be a fast submerged transit. The powerful reactor would deliver near maximum power round the clock. We would not slow except to extend our whip above the water to receive high-priority radio traffic at infrequent intervals. The automatic pilot kept us on course as we plunged northward —straight as an arrow.

At 0822 Nautilus logged her 40,000th league (120,000th mile) on nuclear power. We had doubled Jules Verne's dream, but the historic milestone slipped by uncelebrated. All hands were concentrating on the larger objective which lay ahead.

Life on board Nautilus settled into a familiar pattern, a repetitive cycle of watch-standing, sleeping, working, and eating. Tom Curtis and George Bristow of North American Aviation were busy with Nautilus technicians Rockefeller and

Lerich "peaking up" the inertial navigation system, nursing it as though it were a sick child. Dr. Lyon and Archie Walker checked the ice detection equipment. Throughout the ship other men did the thousand and one things necessary to insure, as far as humanly possible, that no equipment failure would delay or endanger us.

That day the first edition of our daily newspaper was published, entitled "The Panama-Arctic-Pearl Shuttle-Boat News". The acey-deucy and cribbage tournaments were in full swing, and the juke box played constantly. The records had all been changed and most of them recalled our idyllic stop-over in Hawaii. The movies were particularly good. Our friends in Pearl Harbour had chosen them with care.

Twenty-four hours out of Honolulu we received our first ice-summary message, relayed to us by special arrangement from Pearl Harbour. It indicated that conditions were greatly improving, both in the shallow Chukchi Sea and along the coast of Alaska near Point Barrow. On the following day we again slowed to see if there were radio messages for Nautilus. There was one. It was of great importance to Engineman First Class Harry Hedin. It announced that he was a father for the third time—an eight-pound baby girl named Clara. Mrs. Hedin and Clara were fine. Hedin received congratulations all around. I wondered what Clara would think when she was old enough to understand where her father was when she was born.

The shores of Hawaii were soon far behind us, as we steamed ever northward toward the Bering Strait and to an entirely different world from the one we had left four weeks before. Our reactor, the powerful source of energy that drove us, gave us light, cooked for us, and shaved us, performed silently and majestically. Watch-standers scanned networks of instruments, each of which had a vital story to tell about how our magnificent ship was performing. Ours was a world of supreme faith—faith in instruments, faith in the laws of physics, faith in each other and in Him who guided our destiny in the unknown seas ahead.

The submerged run from Pearl Harbour to the Aleutian

chain was completed late on the evening of Saturday, July 26. Cautiously we rose to periscope depth and trained our radar on Yunaska Island. Although we were still twenty miles from land, we established our precise position with a momentary exposure of our masts. Then we went deep to run directly through the channel between Yunaska and Herbert Islands. Midway through, we came up and took another positive check with the periscope radar.

It was foggy and overcast on the surface. Occasionally the Conning Officer, peering through the cross hairs of number one periscope, was able to make out Yunaska Island through the rifts in the fog. His bearings were rough but adequate. Soon we left the bleak, dreary world above and cruised at high speed, taking advantage of the remaining deep water. Shortly we arrived once again in the Bering Sea.

As seen through the periscope, the sea was considerably different from that of the mid-Pacific. It gradually shifted from the clear, warm blue of the tropics to cold, hazy green. No longer did crisp, clean white-caps ride on beautiful, deep blue swells. The caps were transformed to whitish-grey, and they tumbled at the crest of the steep, threatening, sombre seas which marched in procession before the wind. Fat orange-billed puffins waited until our periscope was nearly upon them, then fruitlessly attempted to take off. Others—those off to one side—sat quietly ducking their heads underwater, perhaps to see or hear the big grey shape passing swiftly below them.

As Sunday began, we were still in deep water speeding north toward the narrow Strait. Our talented sonar team—Chief Michaud, Norris, Charette, and Gaines—spent the morning adjusting their equipment, preparing for the tough route that lay ahead.

Shortly after midday we were, once again, due west of our seal preserve, the Pribilof Islands. We changed course to the north to skirt St. Matthew Island. Then in mid-afternoon, when we crossed the hundred-fathom curve, our honeymoon ended. I decreased speed to eighteen knots and rose to 150 feet. It is astonishing still to reflect that though other ships could have

K

come so far and so fast, most of them, by then, would have been very short of fuel. We still had over five thousand miles before we reached our next port, and we would cruise many more thousands before our nuclear fuel was replenished.

That evening the committee for the delayed North Pole celebration again met behind locked doors. I had no idea what they were cooking up, but I was sure it would be appropriate and original. McNally, our cartoonist, magician, and hypnotist, was chairman of the committee. There was avid interest, too, in the contest for designing the flag in honour of our voyage and for the best honorary designation for submerged North Pole visitors. We needed something that equalled—or surpassed—the orders of Bluenoses and Shellbacks. The fact that the prizes were seventy-two-hour liberties in Europe may help explain some of the interest.

When we entered the cold Siberian currents, the sea-water temperature dropped rapidly. Not long afterwards we crossed the twenty-five-fathom curve and I slowed to ten knots. The Navigator obtained a fix on St. Lawrence Island. Siberia was clearly visible off the port beam. The sea was flat calm. Late in the afternoon we came to periscope depth to check for ice. We were cruising in almost exactly the same area in which we had encountered the heavily ridged, landfast ice that had forced us to retreat from the western door on the first trip. Happily, no ice was in sight.

Suddenly our long-range sonar picked up a ship contact several miles to the south-east. I slowed and turned the periscope for a quick look. It was not an American vessel. A two-second observation confirmed what sonar had reported—type of ship, course, speed, and bearing. We returned to cruising depth immediately. I did not want to risk having my periscope spotted.

At 0100 on the morning of July 29, Lieutenant Bill Lalor, the Conning Officer, brought Nautilus to periscope depth. Shep Jenks obtained a fix on Fairway Rock (Krawczyk took a picture of the forbidding hunk of granite through the periscope) and the Diomede Islands. We were very close to the mouth of the Strait. As we aimed for the narrow slot, I ordered full speed ahead.

In time and with ease, we entered the Strait. As I looked at the rugged coast of Siberia, I marvelled at the contrast to the lush shore of Hawaii we had coasted six days before. I turned to the Navigator and asked him to give me the distance, time, and speed from Pearl Harbour. He had already calculated it: 2,901 miles in six days, four hours, and nine minutes; average speed, including passage through 483 miles of shallow water, 19.6 knots. It was a record run. No other submarine then operational could duplicate it; relatively few surface vessels had the speed and endurance to better it.

Once again our sleek bow cut into the waters of the Chukchi Sea. Where before it was jammed with deep draft ice, now it was clear. As we ripped along over the forty miles of shoal water that had caused us so many anxious, zigzagging moments on the previous trip, someone summed up the feelings of all of us: "a piece of cake".

Later that evening Lieutenant Steve White, Engineer Officer on watch, reported a short circuit in the ship's electrical system. Short circuits can sometimes lead to fire. For that reason they must be found and eliminated as soon as possible. Immediately the electricians organized a thorough search for the trouble. After two hours they found it: condensation from a cold circulating-water line had dripped on to a small portable heater and penetrated the leads of the plug. It was a small thing, but it could have led to bigger trouble. It was reassuring to know that we then had on board enough emergency breathing apparatus for all hands.

By midnight we had reached latitude 70 degrees 5 minutes north, sixty miles north of the point where we were forced back by heavy ice on our first trip. There were only a few chunks of ice about. We skirted around them, searching for the true polar pack. I studied the ice carefully for almost an hour.

Plainly speaking, it was shabby-looking—dirty, ragged, zagged, highly ridged, and hummocked—nothing like the pure white, relatively level floes we had seen on the Atlantic side during our 1957 cruise. Silently I ran through the saltier part of my vocabulary. My comments were directed at all the so-called Arctic "experts," including myself, who have written so much about the character of sea ice while knowing so little.

The sweeping statements one finds in much of the Arctic literature are a classic of extrapolation!

TWENTY

Searching for a Highway

The problem we faced in the unknown, uncharted Chukchi then was much the same as that we had faced on the first probe: finding water deep enough to permit us to slip beneath the ice and head north.

Far east of us, off Point Barrow, Alaska, we knew there was a valley in the ocean floor—the Barrow Sea Valley—which led northward into the Arctic Basin. Since the polar pack had receded from the Alaskan coast considerably, we also knew that our chances of picking up the valley and using it as a passageway were fairly good. It was out of our way, however, and would require that we cruise very close to land, increasing our chances of detection. It was our hope that we could simply continue north in the Chukchi, feeling our way until we found some undiscovered valley in the bottom.

Wednesday, July 30, began well. The midnight-to-four watch was on station, intently watching the sonar equipment and fathometers, as Nautilus pushed boldly ahead, submerged, at twelve knots. By then we had reached 70 degrees 45 minutes north. The Officer of the Deck maintained a continuous ice watch on the periscope (though it was midnight inside Nautilus it was broad daylight topside), backstopping our electronics equipment. In not many minutes we picked up ice on the port bow and swung to the right—or east—to avoid it. A heavy fog rolled in and we slowed our speed. The sonars indicated that we had penetrated an area covered with small blocks of ice, only a few feet across and lying very low in the water. Lieutenant Lalor labelled these "ice cubes". Recalling the blow a not-too-large ice cube had dealt our periscopes the year before, I ordered the ship stopped. Then we came up slowly to the surface.

I climbed up to the bridge for a first-hand inspection. It was clear that we were in the midst of brash and block, although it was difficult to determine if we had actually reached the edge of the true polar pack. I could see no large pieces of rafted ice; nevertheless, I was reluctant to go plunging under because the water was still quite shallow. On this trip I intended to take it slow and easy until we were certain of ice conditions and other hazards.

I noted then that in surfacing we had caught a small piece of ice on our deck. Thinking it might make a good souvenir of our trip, I ordered a party on deck to recover it. We put the piece of polar ice in our large deep-freeze and many weeks later, in New York, formally presented it to Rear Admiral Rickover. Those who regard Rickover as a ruthless, hard-bitten man should have seen his reaction. His ordinarily gaunt, serious face was wreathed in smiles. He examined the ice with almost childlike delight. I had the feeling, then, that that piece of ice meant more to him than all the rank, the publicity, accolades, and fame that have been showered upon him.

We took advantage of our brief surfacing to repair several of the ice detectors which had flooded out, and to replace one radio antenna which had been carried away on the trip from Pearl Harbour. The air in the ship was freshened, and many of the crew came topside to take a look at our strange world. I was not over-concerned about being detected. We were lying close to the ice. The fog was heavy. It was difficult to imagine a more isolated area.

Within a few minutes we got under way on the surface, searching for deep water. Since we had seen heavy ice to the west, we jogged east about ten miles before turning north. We were certain that we would reach deep water near latitude 73 degrees north. After many hours of steaming at speeds ranging between five and fifteen knots, we reached 72 degrees 24 minutes north. The water was still too shallow to risk a submerged probe. We studied the ice carefully—until a heavy fog rolled in and obscured our view.

Somewhat discouraged, I ordered Nautilus to reverse course. We steamed south, then east, and then north. Again, we found a dead end. When the fog cleared, we noted that the horizon to the west was a solid mass of ice. The water to the north and east was clear. We increased speed to fifteen knots and steered a north-easterly course. As we moved along, I studied the ice lying to the west of us.

Some of it was nearly coal black in colour. Evidently it was shore ice formed near land whence it picked up a cargo of dirt. Irregular in shape, some of the chunks were as much as forty feet high. That meant that the keels probably projected 120 feet below the surface. Needless to say, I had no desire to sandwich Nautilus between this black ice and the bottom. We had had enough of that on the first trip.

Our Radiomen were busy trying to pick up any messages for Nautilus. They finally received one—our long-sought ice report from Pearl. But it proved disappointing. The aviators had run into low fog along their entire route and, as a result, had little to report. We would have to do our own searching.

We continued nuzzling at the edge of the ice pack, pinging for deep water. We ran into one dead end after another. So many, in fact, that I was mentioned prominently in a song written by a crewman: "The skipper was mad 'cause we couldn't get thru". At length I huddled with Shep Jenks.

"This is impossible," I said. "Let's head east and try the Barrow Sea Valley." In a small way it was admitting defeat, for I was anxious to find any existing valleys in the Chukchi. Time was slipping by, however, and many high-level eyes in Washington were figuratively turned north. All were hoping for not only a successful but speedy polar transit.

Slowly and cautiously we turned south-eastward, edging along the pack boundary towards Point Barrow. Since we were nearing land over which many military planes flew, including our own special ice reconnaissance craft, I directed that a close watch be maintained. An unidentified submarine in those waters, we knew, would cause considerable concern, and might ultimately compromise the security of the mission.

Several hours later, the Officer of the Deck, Ken Carr, and the Junior Officer of the Deck, Bob Kassel, came down from the bridge dripping wet.

"It's raining steadily up there, Captain," Carr said.

At that, Dr. Lyon, who was taking a break in the Wardroom, sipping a cup of coffee, pricked up his ears.

"Raining?" he said. "In the Arctic area rain is extremely rare. You should feel honoured. Why, you're probably two of only a handful of men who have been rained on in the Arctic."

As they pulled off their sopping wet clothing, I could see that neither Carr nor Kassel was in the mood for such dubious honours.

The rain reminded me of our shipboard slogan: "The sun always shines on Nautilus". The saying had originated at the launching of the ship. On that historic day a heavy fog lay across the Thames River and the Electric Boat Company building yards in Groton. But at the very last moment, just as Mrs. Dwight Eisenhower was about to swing the bottle of champagne against Nautilus' bow, the fog disappeared and bright sunlight bathed the scene. It had happened so quickly and so suddenly that many people present considered it a minor but authentic miracle.

I wondered: was this rare Arctic rain pelting Nautilus an ill omen?

At midday our radar picked up an aircraft, and we slipped below the surface of the water to avoid detection. Our Sonarmen immediately reported strange and weird sounds from their instruments. A school of walruses had surrounded us. As we continued south, they tagged along close aboard, no doubt wondering what strange monster had come to disturb their shallow, virtually private sea.

Our progress was slow. Long, rugged fingers of ice, blown down from the pack by the north wind, frequently loomed in our path, causing us to alter course radically. On one occasion we became trapped between two of these peninsulas and, in trying to thread our way to clear water, we were forced to take a long and tedious detour to the north. Later that evening we again found ourselves among ice cubes, with a fog rapidly closing in. A feeling of gloom pervaded the ship. I ordered Nautilus to the surface so that we could proceed—albeit slowly—without endangering the periscopes.

Minor mechanical difficulties were reported. Among these, the most pressing was the fact that our garbage disposal unit (GDU), a ten-inch tube that protrudes from the scullery through the bottom of the ship to the sea, was jammed. The garbage ejector works very much like a torpedo tube. There is an outer and an inner door. When the outer door is shut, keeping out sea water, the inner door can be opened. Garbage bags are placed in the tube. Then the inner door is closed, the outer door opened, and the garbage pushed out by pumping water into the top of the tube. Since the ship could easily be flooded through the GDU tube, it is equipped with a complex interlocking system which prevents the opening of both inner and outer doors at the same time.

The garbage ejector, our only means of disposing of refuse beneath the ice, had failed the year before on our trip under the ice, causing great inconvenience. We had 116 men aboard this time, each one eating three meals a day. The refuse from 348 meals a day is not inconsiderable. I was determined to avoid a repetition of that messy situation, so I ordered the Damage Control Officer, Lieutenant Steve White, to take the necessary action to repair the unit.

White and his repair gang entered the compartment, consisting of the Crew's Mess, Chief Petty Officers' Lounge, and Officers' Wardroom, shut off all ventilation and closed the doors, making it absolutely watertight. Then they turned on the emergency air system and built up pressure inside the compartment until it was slightly more than enough to prevent any entry of sea water. (In the Crew's Mess, the acey-deucy, chess, and cribbage games continued—you can't drive a submariner away with a little air pressure.) The interlocks on the GDU were broken, and with the air pressure holding back the salt water, Frank Skewes and John McGovern probed the tube and soon found the source of trouble: two bags of garbage jammed in the outer door. These bags were quickly removed; the interlocks were replaced, and the air pressure released from the compartment.

To ensure proper loading and operation of the ejector during our polar transit, a garbage disposal team was organized. Once a day the Supply Officer, Lieutenant Bill Cole, and Chief Skewes would report to supervise the Duty Cook and the Mess Cooks when they needed to use the GDU. On the first day, with all that supervision staring him in the face, Commissaryman Second Class Tom Deane declared that he was thinking seriously of writing a book. His title: "I Was First Loader on a GDU".

The remainder of the "night" passed slowly, as we cautiously felt our way toward Point Barrow. The sea was calm, but cluttered with maverick ice. Intermittent fog patches further slowed us. At times we could barely maintain steerage-way, and we drifted much further to the south than we liked.

Just north of Point Franklin, Alaska, we established our position by quick radar sweeps. They showed that we had rounded the corner of the pack and were, at last, aimed directly toward the Barrow Sea Valley, our deep-water gateway to the western Arctic Basin.

A few hours later, with ice in sight on our port beam and dead ahead, we reached deep water, deep enough to clear even the largest floes. As we planed below the surface, I said to myself: *This is it. Let's go, go, go!* Through the periscope I caught a last glimpse of the sky. It was a lovely clear morning with a full moon. The sun was rising, and there was a gentle southerly breeze.

We set course north-eastward, along the Sea Valley, toward very deep water. All sonars were manned, and the operators strained to detect deep-draft ice. I watched the fathometer closely. It revealed that the valley floor was growing deep and wide. I was confident that at last we had it made. Hugging the valley, we took Nautilus deep and increased speed to eighteen knots. It was like pulling on to a highroad from a crowded street.

Soon we were well under the true polar pack. With all preparations made, and the ship finally in her true medium—deep water—and with all equipment working perfectly, at 0852 on August 1, on the 155th meridian, I gave orders to Helmsman David Greenhill: "Come left to north." Dead ahead, 1,094 miles distant, lay the North Pole; eight hundred miles beyond that lay the Greenland-Spitsbergen edge of the pack where, if all went well, we would make our exit.

TWENTY-ONE

"Fan-damn-tastic"

Peary describes the polar pack near the North Pole as a "trackless, colourless chaos of broken and heaved-up ice". Sir John Ross had this to say: "But let them remember that sea ice is stone, a floating rock in the stream, a promontory or an island when aground, not less solid than if it were a land of granite." They were right. But little did they dream of Nautilus, U.S. Navy, nuclear power, 1958.

Saturday morning, August 2, found 116 people running along at four hundred feet at cruising speed on course 000 true, just about forty-four hours short of culminating the most thrilling and adventurous cruise any sailor ever embarked upon. Overhead the ice was almost solid and incredibly rough, projecting downward as much as sixty-five feet from the surface, but averaging ten to fifteen feet thick. It would be less than honest to say that one can submarine under it with total abandon.

At first Frank Adams and I stood "watch and watch," which meant that one of us was up and about at all times. When my co-skipper took over, I could turn in for a few hours of sleep, knowing that the ship was in experienced and capable hands.

As we plunged deeper under the pack, I thought: *Where is the point of no return? Here? A hundred miles from here? A day's journey away? At the Pole itself, perhaps?* Frankly, I did not know. But I had computed it to be at the "Pole of Inaccessibility," the geographic centre of the ice pack, about four hundred miles below the true Pole. But who cared? We were safe, warm, and comfortable in our home beneath the sea.

Morale was high and excitement at fever pitch. Once we had reached deep water beneath the pack, all hands felt that from then on out it was a run for "home". Although our ship's log read eighteen knots, Chief Machinist's Mate Stuart Nelson, who by then was nicknamed "Stop Leak," scampered forward from the Engine Room to ask if the engineers couldn't make "just a couple more going-home turns". I ordered twenty knots. The whole ship seemed to purr along contentedly.

"Boy, this is the way to explore," remarked Robert N. Jarvis, Hospitalman First Class. Pipe in hand, a cup of coffee beside him, he took his ease between atmosphere analyses. "Pinging up and down and all around at twenty knots, fresh air all day long, a warm boat, and good hot food—we sure have the situation in hand. I'd hate to walk across these ice fields up there to the Pole the way Admiral Peary did it."

Though most of us considered the North Pole a desirable objective, our primary mission was to cross from the Pacific Ocean to the Atlantic Ocean, blazing a new north-west passage. Actually, from the standpoint of compass performance, it might have been preferable to avoid the Pole, to ease around it at lower latitude. However, the route across the Pole was the shortest and fastest. Besides, who could resist the temptation to cross the North Pole when it was so close at hand?

Dr. Lyon remained glued to his sonar equipment hour after hour, watching the recording pens trace the contour of the underside of the ice. His new instruments displayed the ice in far greater detail, and with much greater accuracy, than the machines we had used in 1957. In fact, it was at this point that we discovered that the ice pack was far thicker than we had estimated in 1957, and that pressure ridges (ice forced downward when two massive floes press against one another) projected down to 100 or 125 feet. As we sped along, Dr. Lyon's instruments collected in each hour more precise data on the ice and the Arctic Basin floor than have been assembled in all history. When he finally left the ship, he had accumulated two trunkfuls of data.

And what of peaks rising abruptly from the uncharted ocean floor? Our detection equipment kept a sharp "eye" on these obstacles. We found several. At latitude 76 degrees 22 minutes north, in a region where there are no charted soundings, our fathometer, which had been running along fairly steadily at about 2,100 fathoms, suddenly spiked up to 1,500 fathoms, and then, to my concern, to less than 500.

I camped alongside the fathometer for several hours, intently watching the rugged terrain as it unfolded beneath us. I saw incredibly steep cliffs—undersea ranges—rise thousands of feet above the ocean floor. Several times I ordered speed slackened, then resumed, as a promontory levelled off or descended as rapidly as it had risen. The shape of these undersea mountains appeared phenomenally rugged, and as grotesque as the craters of the moon.

As I paced from instrument to instrument, Chief Hospitalman Aberle arrived with the latest atmosphere analysis. He reported our air vitalization machines were working well enough to maintain an atmosphere averaging 20 to 30 parts per million carbon monoxide, 1.0 to 1.5 per cent carbon-dioxide, and between 20 and 21.5 per cent oxygen. These figures were all within, or below, safe limits.

At latitude 83 degrees 20 minutes north we passed abeam of the geographical centre of the ice pack, the "Ice Pole" or "Pole of Inaccessibility". Before the day of nuclear-powered submarines, the name was probably fitting. It may now have to be changed.

It has been reported that, for the crew, Nautilus "hung motionless in time and space". Nothing could be further from the truth. Every man aboard was acutely aware of our rapid and inexorable movement north. As the hours passed, each watch squad gasped at our astounding progress. Men remained transfixed at the electronic machines clocking our track mile by mile, or before the television set on which they could watch the ice passing overhead like beautiful moving clouds. A mixture of suspense, anticipation, and hope was discernible throughout the ship. Few could sleep. Many of us had been praying for the successful attainment of our goal, and now, God willing, it appeared within our reach.

Our psychiatrist, Dr. Kinsey, went about his work methodically and mysteriously, probing, I suppose, for those men who were afraid. Each day, to a random group of volunteers, he distributed cards containing a series of questions, such as "Do you feel happy?" If a man did not feel happy, he was supposed to indicate by writing a single "V" on the card. If he felt slightly happy, he wrote "VV". Three V's meant that he was in fine spirits, and four V's signified total enchantment. Personally, it made no sense to me. I was not one of the select volunteers.

The main fear within me was that which we all shared: a material failure, such as that which occurred in 1957, which would force us to turn back. Every man on board examined and re-examined his instruments and equipment. Vigilance, they all knew, would prevent a small fault from becoming a casualty that would terminate the voyage or leave us stranded beneath the ice.

I did not—could not—sleep. I wandered restlessly about the ship, occasionally taking a peek through the periscope. I was surprised on these observations to see phosphorescent streaks in the water. This is a phenomenon common in tropical waters. It seemed unusual to me to find these streaks in water so cold that the outside of our Engine Room sea-water pipes was covered with thick layers of rime ice.

As I walked about the ship, getting the measure of the crew, I listened as the men spun tales and cracked jokes.

One crewman, recalling the time when Nautilus paid a memorable visit to New Orleans, captivated his shipmates with this story:

"I was headed back for the ship early in the morning. We'd spent most of the evening in the Monkey Bar in the French Quarter. Well, it's about dawn, and I'm walking down this deserted street. Suddenly, out of the corner of my eye, I saw a panhandler crossing the street headed full speed in my direction. He stopped me and asked for a quarter. I looked this bird in the eye and said, 'Look, bud. I'm working this side of the street. You stay on your own side.' Well, I wish you could have seen his face. He was really shook.''

In another compartment, two crewmen on watch were talking.

"Joe, do you know who man's best friend is?" Bill asked.

"Well, I always heard it was a dog," Joe said.

"That's not so," Bill said.

"Well, if the dog isn't, then who is?" Joe asked.

"Lady alligators," Bill explained. "You see, every year these lady alligators come up on the beach and they lay about 1,000 eggs. Then, they tell me, the lady alligator turns around and devours about 999 of the eggs she laid."

"How does that make her man's best friend?" asked Joe.

"Well, Joe, it's like this. If that lady alligator didn't eat those 999 eggs, we'd be up to our neck in alligators."

In spite of this light-hearted talk, every man was alert for an emergency. The leads or polynias were infrequent, but the position of each was carefully plotted, so that if it became necessary to surface, we would know where to find an opening. James H. Prater stood watch in the Torpedo Room, carefully bleeding just the right amount of oxygen into the hull. Nearby was Richard M. Jackman, prepared to make all torpedo tubes ready on an instant's notice, if it became necessary to blast a hole through the ice. We were ready, but the possibility of a casualty seemed remote. Indeed, I had never seen the ship's machinery function so perfectly. Our "out of commission" list reached a new low. It was as if Nautilus herself had found peace and contentment beneath the ice. If she could have filled out one of Dr. Kinsey's cards, it would have contained four V's, or five, or six, for every question.

Shortly after midnight, August 3, we passed latitude 84 degrees north. Since we had entered compass-baffling waters, we made preparations to guard against longitude roulette. At that time we placed our auxiliary gyrocompass in a directional gyro mode so that instead of seeking north, it would tend to seek the line we were following, a Great Circle course up the

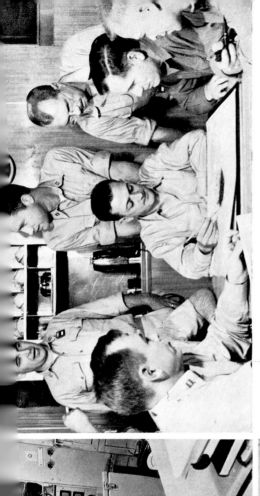

(*above left*) Checking the inertial navigational system, used in obtaining the exact position of Nautilus under the North Pole.

(*above right*) Commander Anderson briefing his officers on polar ice conditions.

(*left*) As Nautilus enters shoal water under the ice, the fathometer is constantly watched.

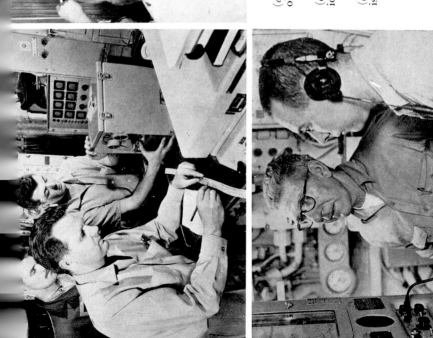

Before members of the crew Commander Anderson signs the letter in which he tells President Eisenhower of the polar crossing.

Western Hemisphere, across the Pole, and south again to the Eastern Hemisphere. This was the track I intended to cruise. When our master gyrocompass began to lose its north-seeking ability, as it would when we approached the northernmost point on earth, then we intended to shift to the auxiliary. Thus we would have something to steer by in the darkness below— something to lead us out on our track south.

In order to ensure that all of the gyrocompasses remained properly oriented, we made all course, speed, and depth changes extremely slowly. For example, when we came near the surface to decrease water pressure on the hull (this is desirable in operating the garbage ejector), we rose with an angle of one or two degrees, instead of the usual twenty to thirty degrees. Once we changed course twenty-two degrees. So gradual was the shift that six minutes elapsed before we had settled on the new heading. Some wag had suggested that when we neared the Pole we might put the rudder hard over and make twenty-five tight circles, thus becoming the first ship in history to circle the earth non-stop twenty-five times. Any such manoeuvre was, of course, out of the question.

As we rapidly closed in on the North Pole, Tom Curtis, manning the inertial navigator, which constantly plotted our position by electronics, made minute adjustments to ensure that his complex instrument was operating properly. At 1000 we crossed latitude 87 degrees north, breaking our record of last year, and with the passing of each new mile, we moved farther north than any other ship in history.

Two hours south of the Pole, a wave of unchecked excitement swept through Nautilus. Every man was up and about, and unabashedly proud to be aboard. Frank Adams, staring intently at the electronic gear, uttered a word often employed by Nautilus men who have exhausted all ordinary expressions to sum up their reaction to the never-ending Nautilus triumphs: "Fan-damn-tastic."

TWENTY-TWO

Piercing the Pole

When we crossed the Pole, of course, no bells would ring, nor would we feel a bump. Only our instruments could tell us how close we had come. Since we had made the decision to cross the Pole, we were determined to hit it precisely on the nose. Along with Navigator Shep Jenks and his assistant, Chief Petty Officer Lyle B. Rayl, I had stationed myself in the Attack Centre, and although we were almost as far north as man can go on this planet, we were literally sweating over the charts and electronic position-indicators, making minute, half-degree adjustments at the helm.

The hour by Nautilus clocks, which were still set on Seattle time, was 1900, or seven o'clock in the evening. Our nuclear engine, which up to then had pushed Nautilus more than 124,000 miles, was purring smoothly. Our electronic log, or speedometer needle, was hovering about twenty knots, the depth gauge needle about four hundred feet. Our sensitive sonar indicated that the endless polar ice pack was running between eight and eighty feet thick. Above the ice, we imagined, the polar wind was howling across its trackless, barren stamping ground, grinding massive floes one upon the other.

By then we had been under ice for sixty-two hours. Obviously, it was not possible to take the usual fix on heavenly bodies to determine our position, so we were navigating primarily by dead reckoning. This means that we were spacing our speed and course on the chart and plotting our position every half-hour or so, accordingly. Our bottom soundings, sometimes useful in submerged navigating, did not help, of course, in this uncharted, unsounded area. Our precision fathometer had indicated differences of as much as eight thousand feet at those rare points where soundings were made, so we could not rely on it. Our only check on our navigating was the inertial navigator. At the exact moment we crossed the Pole, we knew, the instrument would give a positive indication. Tom Curtis moved closer to his dials and scopes as we drew near.

A mile south of the Pole, I told Jenks to inform me when we were four-tenths of a mile from the Pole as indicated by the electronic log. The mileage indicator was moving rapidly. It was only a matter of seconds. Nautilus crewmen had gathered in the Attack Centre and the Crew's Mess.

On Jenks' mark, I stepped up to the mike of the ship's public-address system:

"All hands—this is the Captain speaking. . . . In a few moments Nautilus will realize a goal long a dream of mankind—the attainment by ship of the North Geographic Pole. With continued Godspeed, in less than two days we will record an even more significant historic first: the completion of a rapid transpolar voyage from the Pacific to the Atlantic Ocean.

"The distance to the Pole is now precisely four-tenths of a mile. As we approach, let us pause in silence dedicated with our thanks for the blessings that have been ours during this remarkable voyage—our prayers for lasting world peace, and in solemn tribute to those who have proceeded us, whether in victory or defeat."

The juke box was shut off, and at that moment a hush literally fell over the ship. The only sound to be heard was the steady staccato of pinging from our sonars steadily watching the bottom, the ice, and the dark waters ahead.

I glanced again at the distance indicator, and gave a brief countdown to the crew. "Stand by. 10 . . . 8 . . . 6 . . . 4 . 3 . . . 2 . . . 1. MARK! August 3, 1958. Time, 2315 (11:15 P.M. Eastern Daylight Saving Time). For the United States and the United States Navy, the North Pole." I could hear cheers in the Crew's Mess.

I looked anxiously at Tom Curtis. He was smiling. The inertial navigator had switched precisely as expected, positively confirming that we had crossed the exact North Pole. Curtis sang out: "As a matter of fact, Captain, you might say we came so close we pierced the Pole."

I stood for a moment in silence, awe-struck at what Nautilus had achieved. She had blazed a new submerged nort-hwest passage, vastly decreasing the sea-travel time for nuclear submarines from the Pacific to the Atlantic, one that could be used even if the Panama Canal were closed. When and if nuclear-powered cargo submarines are built, the new route would cut 4,900 miles and thirteen days off the route from Japan to Europe. Nautilus had opened a new era, completely conquered the vast, inhospitable Arctic. Our instruments were, for the first time, compiling an accurate and broad picture of the Arctic Basin and its approaches. Nautilus' achievement was dramatic proof of United States leadership in at least one important branch of science; and it would soon rank alongside or above the Russian sputnik in the minds of millions. Lastly, for the first time in history a ship had actually reached the North Pole. And never had so many men—116—been gathered at the Pole at one time.

I was proud of what Nautilus had done, yet I felt no sense of personal triumph or achievement. That we had reached the Pole was the work and support of many people. My reaction, frankly, was an overwhelming feeling of relief that after months and months of preparation and two unsuccessful probes we had finally made it.

Precisely at the Pole, for the record, I made note of some statistics which may or may not prove useful. The water temperature was 32.4 degrees Fahrenheit. The depth of the sea was 13,410 feet, exactly 1,927 feet deeper than reported by Ivan Papanin, a Russian who landed there, he claims, in an airplane in 1937. (In 1909 Admiral Peary had found the depth "greater than 9,000 feet".) At the exact Pole our ice detectors noted a pressure ridge extending twenty-five feet down.

After crossing the Pole, I made my way forward to join in the "North Pole Party" in the Crew's Mess. My first act was to pay modest tribute to the man who, more than any other, had made our historic voyage possible: the President of the United States. A few minutes before, I had written him a message. It concluded: "I hope, sir, that you will accept this letter as a memento of a voyage of importance to the United States." In the Mess, before seventy crew members of Nautilus, I signed this letter, and one to Mrs. Eisenhower, who had christened the ship.

Other events followed. A "North Pole" cake, prepared especially by Leading Commissaryman Jack L. Baird, was cut, distributed, and wolfed down. Electrician's Mate First Class James Sordelet raised his right hand and became the first man in history to re-enlist at the North Pole. In a special North Pole ceremony eleven other men, having passed the rigid written and oral examinations, were "qualified in nuclear submarines". The prize-winning title to correspond to Shellbacks and Bluenoses was announced: Panopo, short for "Pacific to the Atlantic via the North Pole." A "North Pole" post card, stamped with the special North Pole cachet, was distributed to all hands. On the reverse side was a cartoon by McNally

The franking on the "North Pole" mail

showing a sailor in a bathing suit standing on a small block of ice leaning against a striped "North Pole". The card read: "Greetings from Sunny Panama." All during these proceedings, movie and still cameras whirred and clicked.

Then a distinguished citizen "came aboard". It was our talented McNally, dressed as Santa Claus. What a sight he made! Red vegetable colouring was plastered on his face. His whiskers were made of medical cotton, and a pillow was stuffed inside his Santa Claus suit, made of flag bunting.

Santa berated us for entering his private domain during the vacation season. He chided us particularly for our failure to abide by his restriction on the use of garbage disposal units by submerged Pole-crossing submarines! I pleaded ignorance and promised on behalf of all the ship's company children to abide by all his rules henceforth.

That done, Santa Claus relaxed and became his usual jovial self. He listened very patiently as one of the fathers in the crew, Chief Engineman Hercules H. Nicholas, argued that the behaviour of our children was absolutely beyond reproach. Santa promised, in light of our personal visit to the North Pole, that the coming Christmas season would be merry and lucrative for all our children.

Perspiring heavily, Santa finally said, "Well, I've got to go back to the Pole to make sure the elves are working." And with that our extraordinary party ended. The juke box was turned back on; men drifted to their bunks for a little rest.

An "extra" edition of the ship's newspaper was published that day, entitled "Nautilus Express—North Pole Edition." It was unusually mild in tone and contained nothing libellous, which is an indication, I believe, that all hands were deeply moved by Nautilus' triumph. The feeling of the crew was summed up in an article by the paper's editor, John H. Michaud.

He wrote:

At NAUTILUS' Greatest Moment

The crew of the USS Nautilus (SS(N)571) have at this time accomplished one of the greatest feats that is possible for a peaceful nation composed of average citizens. We have reached a point that has never been attained before this time. Many courageous men have tried, few succeeded. Of all those men that have tried we humbly ask their forgiveness. They had courage and fortitude that many of us never had, never will have in our lifetime. To those men this is dedicated. We have arrived at the North Pole. The very last region of the earth that has never been explored. True we came to this region in a habitat that is not normal for man. We came with the best equipment, the best men, and a relatively new form of power. Without this power we would have never attained the goal we set out for, now that we have reached that goal this same power will take us home to our loved ones, who have endured many hardships that will never be told to us. They bid us goodbye, some with tears, others with a strained look and always a question in their eyes. Is it this time? They know the goal that we have been striving for, since our return of last year, but the time and place we cannot say. We have left our loved ones not unlike the explorers of other times, with prayers to bring us Godspeed and a safe return. We are on that return now with much rejoicing and many happy thoughts for those we left behind. To my fellow shipmates this has been one of the most enjoyable trips I have ever been on, and without a doubt the most important. May God be with you on all other voyages that you make.

TWENTY-THREE

"Nautilus 90 North"

Although one goal—the North Pole—had been achieved, we had yet another and even more significant one to realize: the first complete transpolar voyage from the Pacific to the Atlantic. The long leg of the journey was done. If all continued to go well, we would reach open water in the Greenland-Spitsbergen portal within a day and a half.

Without changing course we were now heading due south. The master compass was secured and slewed around. Slowly it began to settle on the new meridian. The auxiliary gyro still indicated course north because, as a directional gyro, it was simply pointing out in space, rotating at the same rate as the earth. How the Helmsmen complained to find themselves steering south by a compass that still pointed north!

I had been requested by the Chief of Naval Operations to send him a brief message after we crossed the Pole—if we could find a polynia or lead large enough to permit us to surface. I drafted the message. It was short and to the point: "Nautilus 90 North." We searched in vain for a polynia. The ice overhead was deep, thick, and closely packed. I stuffed the Top Secret message in my pocket.

With life on board Nautilus once again slipping into a familiar routine, we hurried on at better than twenty knots, making "liberty turns" as the sailors call it when headed toward port. By 0700, August 4, with the Pole 240 miles behind us, the master gyro at last settled on the true meridian. Our Helmsman, Daniel Brigman, breathed a sigh of relief. Now on course south he could actually steer south. The inertial navigator continued to check perfectly with our "dead reckoning position".

After the master gyro had settled and appeared to be operating perfectly, I felt safe in ordering a change in course. I asked the Navigator for a heading to the opening between Spitsbergen and Greenland. It was not a simple request. In order to steer an accurate course, we would have to change our heading one

The message announcing the crossing of the Pole

degree for each degree of longitude that we crossed. Because the longitudinal lines were so very close together (they converge completely, of course, at the true geographic Pole), we computed that there would be twenty-six changes—one every twenty minutes. So be it!

That evening, according to our "dead reckoning" navigator, Nautilus entered waters that we had probed on our 1957 cruise. Our charts were covered with soundings—those that we had compiled on our first trip under the ice. Oddly enough, the readings on our fathometer did not match those on the chart. A slight uneasiness permeated the navigation party. After studying the information available, I concluded that we were west and north of our dead reckoning position. Therefore, I ordered a slow course change that would aim us slightly east of south—towards Spitsbergen.

A few hours later, at 0400 on August 5, we cruised under a small patch of open water. Soon afterwards our sonars picked up a giant ice floe measuring twelve miles from stem to stern.

"Are you certain?" I asked, making a bee-line for the sonar instrument. This kind of ice was not at all typical of the ice we had encountered in this region the year before. Then it had been mostly block and brash—not twelve-mile floes!

At that moment our fathometers registered 2,400 fathoms—a depth far greater than the reports we had been receiving, or had observed on our trip the year before. I glanced at the chart. The only sounding approaching 2,400 fathoms was near the Pole. I wondered: Had our equipment failed? Had we been running in circles? It seemed impossible. Too many things were checking. I shrugged off my concern, thinking we had simply discovered another weird ice characteristic—and one more new hole in the ocean floor.

However, a few moments later, we received from the bathy-thermograph another startling—or, I should say, downright unnerving—report, indicating that the outside sea-water temperature was getting not warmer, as we had expected on our run south, but colder. In a flash our uneasiness built up to genuine apprehension. *We couldn't possibly be near northern Greenland*, I thought. *By now we would already have run aground!* A terrible—now ridiculous—thought crept into my mind: *Have we actually been trapped in a game of longitude roulette? Are we coming into some strange sea? Possibly the East Siberian Sea?*

While I was pondering those questions, the Conning Officer reported that we had just passed under a patch of clear blue water. I raced for the periscope. Through the glass I could see a steady intensity of blue-green. Completely absorbed, I studied the water. One minute passed—then five—then ten. Meanwhile, the detection equipment reported "all clear overhead".

I ordered speed slackened and we ascended to periscope depth slowly—just in case we had been fooled by a thin layer of ice. I stopped the ship and then backed down. Up went the starboard whip antenna—our "ice pick". We inched toward the surface. Through the scope I could see wave motion. Then the periscope broke the surface, and brilliant sunlight streamed into the glass.

As I backed away, temporarily blinded by the glare, Lieutenant Ken Carr said, "Captain. The sun always shines on Nautilus."

I scanned the surface of the water carefully, noting several small chunks of ice. But there were no large floes. Reluctant to expose the periscope to possible damage, and anxious to give the Radiomen as much antenna height as possible, I ordered the ship surfaced.

From the size of the waves and the swells, we were certain that we were in an open sea. The water seemed similar to that we had encountered in the Greenland Sea in 1957. As we carefully scrutinized the ice, bending around us to the west and south, we tentatively concluded that we had reached the edge of the pack. Although we were fairly sure of our position, I have learned that in polar navigation it is best to have clear proof. I waited anxiously as the navigators computed our position by observations of the sun.

We worked our way south, meanwhile, dodging a very large floe, evidently one that had become detached from the pack. In contrast to the dirty floes we had seen on the other side, the ice was brilliantly white. We passed a small seal lazing in the sun atop a small, private chunk of ice that had torn loose from a floe. As we rushed by, the seal seemed not in the least surprised or disturbed. In fact, he behaved as though he saw submarines emerging from the polar pack every day.

After about an hour on the surface, Navigator Jenks reported our exact position which, to the relief of all, placed us just where we thought we were: north-east of Greenland. After the transit of 1,830 miles—ninety-six hours under the ice—we were only a few miles—far less than ten—from his dead-reckoning position. In my opinion, it was the most remarkable piece of ship navigation ever accomplished. I shook my head in amazement and uttered a Nautilus word . . . "Fan-damn-tastic!" Then I passed the word to the crew on the ship's public-address system and made my way down to the Radio Room to see if our message had been sent off.

Communications in the Arctic are, as previously noted, erratic. I found Radiomen Harry Thomas and Terrence Provost flipping switches and adjusting knobs to pull the last ounce of energy out of the transmitter. Using brevity codes, Provost got on the telegraph key and clicked out: "Any U.S. Navy radio station this is an unidentified station with two operational immediate messages." Provost sent the message over and over again, but he could get no response. It was a frustrating experience. Here we were, possessed of momentous news, but no one would listen to us.

"Captain," cracked one of the men, "we should have brought some carrier pigeons with us."

I was on the verge of submerging the ship for a fast run south to a more favourable atmosphere when, finally, a weak signal came through. "This is U.S. Navy radio, Japan. Send V's so I can tune you in." In a few painstaking minutes we fired off our historic three-word message, "Nautilus 90 North." Soon the message was en route to Washington, via Japan.

As Provost shifted to the second message, Japan faded out and another station answered. This time it was U.S. Navy radio, Honolulu. Then Radio Londonderry broke in. We relayed the message to Honolulu and, shortly afterwards, submerged, and set cruising speed for the Denmark Strait. Operation SUNSHINE, perhaps the most remarkable voyage in the history of man, had been completed.

From then on Nautilus moved fast, events even faster.

Months before, when Operation SUNSHINE first evolved, Captain Aurand, the President's Naval Aide, had told me that if the trip proved successful, the White House desired to release the information as rapidly as possible. To expedite the release, an extraordinary plan was drawn up. After Nautilus left the ice pack, she would proceed to a secret rendezvous off Reykjavik, Iceland. (When Navigator Jenks stumbled over the name Reykjavik, one Nautilus sailor said, "Never mind how you pronounce it, just find it.") At that point, unobserved by ships and aircraft, Nautilus would stop and wait for a helicopter. When the helicopter came in sight we were to surface. Then I would leave Nautilus and climb aboard the helicopter, which would fly me to Iceland. There a plane would wait to lift me to Washington, where I would report directly to the President.

My feelings were mixed about this phase of Operation SUNSHINE. This would be an honour excelling all I had ever before experienced, or probably ever would experience in the future. It would provide an opportunity for me to see Bonny, who was waiting at our home in Mystic, Connecticut. It would give the finest Executive Officer in submarines, Frank Adams, a chance to step up, temporarily, to command what we both believe is the finest submarine in the world. My main concern was that during my absence the officers and men of Nautilus would find out that I was completely dispensable!

At dawn on August 7, the helicopter, an Air Force H-19, thrashed into the periscope field. I ordered three blasts on the surfacing alarm, zipped up my coveralls (to conceal my uniform), and slipped on a life jacket. As the bridge hatch cleared the water, Frank Adams assumed command of the ship. The H-19 pilot hovered the craft a scant five feet above our afterdeck. In seconds my gear was aboard. With the help of a crewman on the helicopter and a tall step, so was I.

On board the H-19, wearing flight coveralls, I found a friendly and familiar officer—Captain Peter Aurand. He gave me a warm greeting and a message from the President, which said:

TO THE OFFICERS AND CREW OF
THE NAUTILUS

Congratulations on the magnificent achievement—WELL DONE.

It was signed by Dwight D. Eisenhower.

We handed the message down to a Nautilus crewman. About fifteen minutes later the H-19 landed in Keflavik, directly alongside a Navy transport plane whose engines were turning over. Not more than a minute after that, the transport taxied down the runway and took off. As we moved south at four miles a minute the early morning light faded. My thoughts drifted back to Nautilus, which at that moment was steaming rapidly eastward, deep in the Atlantic, en route to Portland, England. I could visualize her—sleek, grey, shark-like on the outside, shiny, warm, and comfortable on the inside. For a brief moment my mind was flooded with visions of jagged ice profile recordings. And then, for the first time since passing Point Barrow, Alaska, six days before, I found restful sleep.

Soon the wheels of our plane touched down on the runway at Washington National Airport. A car was waiting, which took us to the White House. In another few minutes, to my astonishment, I was face to face with Bonny, who had been flown down from Mystic in another Navy aeroplane. I was still recovering from that surprise when someone whispered in my ear, "The President is waiting."

I was too dazed to be nervous. I presented to President Eisenhower the letters I had written at the North Pole, as well as a special gift to Mrs. Eisenhower from the Nautilus crew: one of the ship's clocks stopped at the exact moment we crossed the Pole: 7.15 P.M. Seattle time. The President was highly pleased, not only with the Nautilus' achievement, but also with the mementos. I replied in effect: "Without your backing, sir, this voyage would never have been possible." It was neither flattery nor an exaggeration. No man knew the truth of it better than I.

We chatted informally for a few moments, then Bonny and I followed the President into a room packed with reporters, photographers, television and movie cameras. There the news of the trip was released, and the President, for the first time in peacetime, awarded the Presidential Unit Citation to a naval vessel.

Captain Aurand read the citation:

> For outstanding achievement in completing the first voyage in history across the top of the world, by cruising under the Arctic ice cap from the Bering Strait to the Greenland Sea. During the period 22 July 1958 to 5 August 1958, U.S.S. NAUTILUS, the world's first atomic powered ship, added to her list of historic achievements by crossing the Arctic Ocean from the Bering Sea to the Greenland Sea, passing submerged beneath the geographic North Pole. This voyage opens the possibility of a new commercial seaway, a north-west passage, between the major oceans of the world. Nuclear powered cargo submarines may, in the future, use this route to the advantage of world trade.
>
> The skill, professional competency and courage of the officers and crew of NAUTILUS were in keeping with the highest traditions of the Armed Forces of the United States and the pioneering spirit which has always characterized our country.

After the press conference Bonny and I drove to Admiral Rickover's office to pay our respects. We found him in a very happy mood. We didn't stay long, for although it was Admiral Rickover's brain child, nuclear power, that had made our momentous voyage possible, he was not anxious to dwell on the feat. His mind was preoccupied with the details and planing of nuclear submarines of the future.

By Sunday, August 10, I was again airborne, en route to England to rejoin the Nautilus at sea just outside Portland. Nearing England, the captain of the Pan American airliner made contact with the Nautilus by radio. I relayed a brief account of the events that had transpired—particularly the astonishing reaction to our trip throughout the world—and inquired of Frank Adams if he had found my bunk soft. The crew, which had tuned the ship's radio to BBC channels, were already up to date. Adams replied that he had not had time to sleep.

On Tuesday, August 12, I boarded a helicopter in Portland and flew out to the ship. Then, making full speed, we steamed into Portland, England, and an overwhelming welcome. After six days in England, we broke the speed record for a submerged crossing to New York, where we were greeted by an armada of tugboats and fire boats. Later, we were honoured by a ticker-tape parade.

Bonny and most of the other Nautilus wives were standing on the pier in New York when we pulled alongside. When I caught sight of them, I thought of a poem our Yeoman, Charles Payne, had written for the special North Pole edition of our ship's newspaper. It was a moving tribute to our wives, whose unselfish devotion, I feel certain, has made many of Nautilus' triumphs possible. I recalled two lines from Payne's poem:

> They ask for nothing—nothing we can't give,
> They just want us home, and a normal life to live.

We were almost home but, it would appear, life is seldom normal for those who serve on Nautilus.

Rear Admiral Rickover being presented with a chunk of polar ice from the Chukchi Sea.

Commander Anderson receiving the Legion of Merit from President Eisenhower at a special White House ceremony.

Daily Mail photos

Nautilus arrives to a tremendous reception at Portland, England. A magnificent feat has been accomplished, and the north-west Passage—the dream of centuries of explorers—is open at last.

Personnel Aboard Nautilus

TRANS-POLAR VOYAGE, AUGUST 1958

Officers and Civilian Technicians

William R. Anderson (Commander)
Frank M. Adams (Lieutenant Commander)
Kenneth M. Carr (Lieutenant)
William S. Cole (Lieutenant)
Richard F. Dobbins (Commander)
Paul J. Early (Lieutenant Commander)
Donald P. Hall (Lieutenant)
John W. Harvey (Lieutenant)
Shepherd M. Jenks (Lieutenant)
Robert H. Kassel (Lieutenant)
Robert L. Kelsey (Lieutenant)
William G. Lalor, Jr. (Lieutenant)
Steven A. White (Lieutenant)
Jack L. Kinsey (Captain)
George G. Bristow
Thomas E. Curtis
Waldo K. Lyon
Archie C. Walker

Enlisted Men

John A. Aberle	Freddie L. Boswell, Jr.
Bruce F. Aquizap	Philip J. Boyle
Jack L. Baird	Donald D. Brady
Ralph D. Barnhart, Jr.	Dennison "K" Breese
Richard T. Bearden	Daniel K. Brigman
Robert D. Bell	James Brown
Nile A. Bergquist	William J. Brown
Charles H. Black	Arthur J. Callahan

Roland L. Cave
Alfred A. Charette, Jr.
Boyd W. Cohenour
Thomas J. Deane
Joseph D. Degnan
Earl R. Diamond
John F. Draper
Edward D. Dunn, Jr.
Wallace M. Durkin
Thomas Emanuel
Leslie F. Evans
Bobby J. Faircloth
Billy G. Fowlks
William G. Furnholm
William A. Gaines
David L. Greenhill
Roger A. Hall
William A. Hansen
Dowell R. Harrell
Walter J. Harvey
Harry D. Hedin
Albert J. Herrera
Joseph R. Higgins
Stonewall J. Hilton
Ernest F. Holland
James G. Irvin
Richard M. Jackman
Robert N. Jarvis
Ronald W. Jett
James H. Johnson
Raymond G. Kazebee
Richard M. King
Ronald L. Kloch
James P. Knotts
John J. Krawczyk
Raymond L. Kropp
John B. Kurrus

Lynus J. Larch
Barry H. Lerich
Allan R. Lewis
David H. Long
Joseph P. Marchand
John P. McGovern
William J. McNally, Jr.
Marvin L. Megason, Jr.
John H. Michaud
Roger R. Miller
James A. Morley
Richard T. Murphy
Stuart Nelson
Hercules H. Nicholas
James R. Norris
William P. O'Neill
Clemente L. Ortega
Charles L. Parshall
Gary L. Patterson
Charles A. Payne
John E. Pendleton
Robert S. Pfeiffer
James T. Phelps
Imon L. Pilcher
James H. Prater
Clarence E. Price
Terrence R. Provost
Lyle B. Rayl
Robert Rockefeller
Robert C. Scott
George E. Shabenas, Jr.
Robert E. Simonini
Frank A. Skewes
Malcolm Snelgrove
James R. Sordelet
Gilbert C. Spurr
Robert C. Stroud

Kirby L. Talley

Harry D. Thomas

Normal A. Vitale

Curtis J. Wagner

Richard J. Williamson

Richard E. Wood

John C. Yuill

John P. Zaretki

Index

Scott, Robert C., 70
Seawolf, 6, 34
Simonini, Robert E., 108
Skate, 87, 88, 90, 92, 112
Skews, Frank A., 154
Smith, Capt. A. C., 89
Sordelet, James R., 165
Spitzbergen, 40, 43, 56, 58, 84, 87, 155, 168, 169, 170
Spurr, Gilbert C., 114
Szarzynski, Theodore, 100

Teixeira, John, 105
Thomas, Harry D., 126, 128, 172
Tonseth, Lieut., 142
Trigger, 54, 57, 64, 65, 69, 73, 77, 79
Triton, 142

United States Submarine School, 20, 21

Verne, Jules, 32, 79, 143
Vitale, Norman A., 114

Wadsworth, Lieut. Frank, 76
Walker, Archie C., 140, 144
Walker, Capt. Frank, 84
Warder, Rear Admiral F. B., 88-90, 130, 134
Watkins, Rear Admiral Frank, 6, 20, 21
White, Lieut. Steven A., 65, 95, 147, 153
Wilkins, Rear Admiral C. W., 43, 53, 57, 58

About the Authors

COMMANDER WILLIAM R. ANDERSON was born at Bakerville, Tennessee, June 17, 1921. He graduated from Columbia Military Academy, Columbia, Tennessee, in 1938, and from the United States Naval Academy in 1942. After schooling at the United States Submarine School in New London, Connecticut, he made eleven war patrols on the U.S. submarines Tarpon, Narwhal, and Trutta. After Word War II he served on the submarines Sarda, Trutta, and Tang, and in 1953 assumed command of the fast attack submarine Wahoo. In June 1957, after a tour of duty under Rear Admiral H. G. Rickover in the Naval Reactors Branch, he assumed command of the atomic-powered submarine Nautilus. While serving under Admiral Rickover, Commander Anderson began studying the Arctic regions and assembling notes and material which form the basis of portions of this book.

Commander Anderson is married to the former Yvonne Etzel. The Andersons have two children, Michael, thirteen, and William, three. They reside in Mystic, Connecticut.

CLAY BLAIR, JR., was born in Lexington, Virginia, May 1, 1925, and was educated in public schools throughout the South. In 1943 he volunteered for the Navy and spent twenty-two months in the submarine service. Serving on the U.S.S. Guardfish, he participated in two war patrols against the Japanese. After the war he attended Tulane and Columbia universities. He joined Time-Life in 1949, and in 1950 was made military correspondent for *Time* and *Life* magazines. He is the author or co-author of four previous books, including *The Atomic Submarine and Admiral Rickover*, the first account of the building of the Nautilus and the life of the admiral who conceived the ship. He has also written many magazine articles on the Nautilus. In March 1957 he joined the staff of *The Saturday Evening Post* as Associate Editor in the Washington office.

Mr. Blair is married to the former Agnes Kemp Devereux. The Blairs have three children, Marie Louise, seven, Clay, III, five, and Joseph, two. They reside in Chevy Chase, Maryland.

FIRST TRIP – JUNE 1958

1   JUNE 9, 1958 – Underway from Seattle

2   JUNE 14 – Landfall at a hundred miles; wishing the water was
        1/100th that deep

3   JUNE 16 – The bottom lies at forty-five, the ice at twenty odd.
        Reversed course for safer passage

4   JUNE 16 – The log that looked like a snorkling submarine

5   JUNE 17 – With the Diomedes in sight, set course through the Bering Strait

6   JUNE 17 – "Captain, will you come in please". The gigantic piece of ice

7   JUNE 18 – Our painful retreat

8   JUNE 28 – Aloha to Oahu and a wonderful impressive welcome